SARAH THOMPSON
STYLE COUNCIL

SARAH THOMPSON

STYLE COUNCIL

Inspirational interiors in ex-council homes

Foreword by Wayne Hemingway, MBE

◙ SQUARE PEG

For my children, Stanley and Betty,
who make anywhere home.
And my parents, Thelma and Roy,
who taught me how to play house.

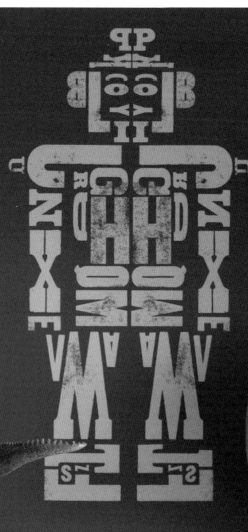

Roberts/Fletcher *Ghoul School*

MATCH OF THE DAY ANNUAL 2013 BBC BOOKS

CHILDREN'S ENCYCLOPEDIA EARTH

AMAZING POP-UP MONSTER TRUCKS  WALKER BOOKS

CONTENTS

FOREWORD

Wayne Hemingway, MBE
HemingwayDesign

I'd never met Sarah, the author of this book, before she emailed me with her proposal for an interiors book about ex-council houses. But when someone sends you an idea for a book about how a new generation are making ex-council stock highly desirable and says they have a (brilliant) idea to call it *Style Council*, then your eyes light up.

The British council house is something I've been engaged with, both personally and professionally, since as far back as I can remember. As a lad I lived in the Queen's Park flats in Blackburn. They went the way of so many: unappreciated by the council and the public, as well as succumbing to concrete cancer. But my memories of Queen's Park are of a spacious, purple shagpile home set in the most amazing landscape that served as a giant adventure playground to me as a boy. So I'd understood from an early age the importance of the generous spirit underpinning much post-war social housing – the idea that homes were places not just to live in a functional sense, but where people could be happy and feel a sense of belonging. Like most sixties social housing, the flats had been built to Parker Morris standards, a set of building guidelines established in 1961 that sought to ensure that everyone could swing a cat in their home. Not that I promote cat swinging, but you couldn't swing a Manx cat in most new-build homes today!

Parker Morris standards and the idea of a generous spirit in home design would come into play later in life in my role as chairman of Building for Life and my current role on the Trustee Board of the Commission for Architecture and the Built Environment at the Design Council, and in the housing and estate design work that my wife Gerardine and I have been involved in across the UK. The generosity and communality of landscape that were the Queen's Park flats

manifested themselves at our career-defining housing development in Gateshead, the Staiths South Bank.

British new-build homes have just about the smallest space standards in Europe, with ex-council housing from the 1960s and '70s being over 30 per cent larger than much of the new housing being built. If space is a luxury, then the sort of council housing that I grew up in is beginning to look like some of the most luxurious housing on the market. And it's hard to escape the irony that, when Margaret Thatcher gave councils the power to sell off their housing with the Right-to-Buy Act in 1980, a move which played a significant role in today's destructive housing shortages, she also inadvertently gave the next generation the chance to access some of the best housing design of the twentieth century.

Now, as I write this foreword, my eldest daughter Tilly – a qualified urban designer – has just had an offer accepted on her first home, an ex-council flat in London. Tilly and many of her peers are actively seeking out these properties, which they see through the eyes of a modern generation, appreciating their clean lines and the natural light and the space they offer. As the homes in this book testify, the ex-council home provides a liveability and adaptability for contemporary life that their Victorian and Edwardian counterparts can't match. The council house has come full circle.

ABOUT THE COUNCIL HOUSE

Catherine Croft
Director, Twentieth Century Society

No one is building council houses any more. But for a brief period from the late 1940s to the mid-1960s, local authority architects' departments were where the best architecture students aspired to work. They were building prolifically, gave young architects huge responsibility and opportunity to shine, and in some cases built radical schemes, driven by enormous idealism.

Most of the homes in this book come from this brief, heroic period of council house construction; some are examples of earlier phases of local authority development. While many of these homes – particularly those on estates – started out as sources of great pride, with tenants eager to move in, by 2007 Lynsey Hanley could confidently assert in her book *Estates, An Intimate History* that 'to anybody who doesn't live on one (and to some who do), the term "council estate" means hell on earth. Estates had come to mean alcoholism, drug addiction,

relentless petty stupidity, a kind of stir-craziness induced by organic poverty…'

What had gone wrong, and why are the homeowners included here defying such stereotypes?

COUNCIL HOUSING: A BRIEF HISTORY

There was social housing in Britain from the latter half of the nineteenth century onwards. Philanthropic Model Dwellings Companies were private firms which built new homes for working-class tenants, at the same time providing private investors with a competitive rate of return.

But until the 1919 (Addison) Housing Act, councils were not major providers of housing. Following the Act, Housing Committees were set up and new subsidies encouraged councils to build. The aim was to provide 'Homes for Heroes', offering a better way of life for soldiers returning from the First World War. Councils constructed cottage estates, inspired by the Garden City Movement, on the edge of town. London County Council's enormous Becontree estate in Dagenham housed over 100,000 people by 1935. The new houses had gas and electric light (but not plug sockets), inside toilets, fitted baths and front and back gardens. There were strict rules about carrying out house and garden maintenance, and on children's behaviour and keeping pets.

The Housing Act of 1930 encouraged mass slum clearance by giving councils powers to buy and demolish privately owned properties. Much of the slum clearance was replaced with walk-up blocks of flats, mostly three to five storeys high. Some were architecturally progressive and technologically innovative, such as the Quarry Hill flats in Leeds, inspired by Karl Marx Hof in Vienna and built of concrete over a steel framework.

The concept of mixed development, estates comprising both high flats for single people, childless couples and the elderly, and family houses and maisonette blocks, was encouraged by the pioneering housing expert, Elizabeth Denby. She toured low-cost housing in Europe, giving a talk in 1936 to the Royal Institute of British Architects (RIBA) on 'Rehousing from the slum dweller's point of view', and published her findings in a book in 1938. She worked with modernist architect Maxwell Fry on schemes which were later to inspire post-war designers.

Housing construction ceased during the Second World War and by 1945 there was an enormous housing shortage. Tackling this shortage was central to the 1945 Labour government's programme of welfare reform, but it was local authorities, rather than central government, who were to take the lead.

In the short term, existing properties were repaired and 'prefabs' developed and erected. Precast concrete panel systems were pioneered to speed up the process of producing conventional-looking two-storey homes. As some of these construction companies, including Wates and Reema, grew larger they extended this approach to multi-storey flats, and finally to high-rise blocks. Providing a high volume of new homes was a priority, with league tables published to encourage Housing Departments to compete with one another.

Architects were now aiming not just to deliver large numbers of housing units, but to create new ways of living, which combined the best of traditional street life with access to fresh air, light and modern amenities.

Most council housing was built in an overtly modern style, but some estates, such as Southwark's Alberta Estate, still incorporated Arts and Crafts-inspired features. Two distinct stylistic trends emerged: a Scandinavian-inspired picturesque 'soft' modernism, and a more robust, craggy aesthetic, inspired by Le Corbusier's post-war Unité buildings, with their board-marked concrete finishes – this developed into a British new brutalism, its most extreme examples represented by the dramatic tower blocks of Ernö Goldfinger, at Trellick Tower (page 127) and Balfron Tower (page 57).

In terms of planning, the major imperative was to improve upon balcony access, which provided little privacy, as neighbours had to walk closely past one another's windows. Denys Lasdun's cluster block of Keeling House (page 75) was dramatic, but very expensive. Easier to replicate at a larger scale were the various versions of 'streets in the sky', much wider access galleries designed to generate their own version of street life – a concept pioneered at Park Hill, Sheffield (page 83). Although building high was more expensive than low or medium-rise, it was increasingly encouraged by government subsidy systems, concerns about loss of farmland, the need to rehouse large numbers on limited inner-city sites and a desire by some slum dwellers to be re-housed as near to their old homes as possible.

How much room did people need to live comfortably? The influential Parker Morris Committee's 1961 report *Homes for Today and Tomorrow* was aspirational and called for generous room sizes, made compulsory for all new town housing from 1967 and all council housing from 1969. They ceased to be compulsory in 1980, when the Local Government, Planning and Land Act sought to reduce costs.

The collapse of Ronan Point, a sys-tem-built block which crumpled like a house of cards after a gas explosion in 1968, is generally credited with calling a halt to high-rise plans, but the Housing Cost Yardstick, introduced the year before, had already tipped the balance in favour of medium-rise schemes, while research at Cambridge University had demonstrated that the same numbers of people could be housed on the same amount of land at lower heights by using stepped sections.

In the decade after 1945, 1.5 million council homes had been completed. And while the majority were in towns and cities, rural authorities were also building. These were often short terraces on the edge of a village, or a group of terraces or semis around a new village green. Some used lo-cal stone, but colour-washed render or brick were cheaper options.

From the 1970s councils built increasing-ly fewer homes. The introduction of the Right-to-Buy under the Housing Act 1980 enabled over one million tenants to buy the houses they were living in at below the mar-ket value. Not surprisingly it was generally

the more popular and conventionally con-structed properties which were purchased. The number of houses managed by London's councils shrank from 840,000 in 1984 to just over 500,000 by the end of the century. As James Meek points out in his book *Private Island*: 'It offered a life-changing fortune to a relatively small group of people, a group that, not by coincidence, contained a large number of swing voters.' Spending restric-tions had been introduced, so the revenue raised could not be used to build replace-ment homes, or used for refurbishment of remaining council properties.

COUNCIL PROPERTIES, PRIVATE OWNERSHIP

Like many of the people whose homes are included in this book, I love my ex-local authority property, but am unhappy about the political and economic circumstances which have brought about the situation I find myself in.

At the Twentieth Century Society, and in previous jobs at English Heritage, I cam-paign for the preservation of the best examples of twentieth-century architecture, including many public housing projects. I passionately believe these are brilliant, innovative design solutions, and ones which we can still learn from today, as we seek to build new housing to combat a worsening housing shortage. Some of the estates we have fought for have been run down. Many have been poorly maintained, but I am con-fident that none of the ones we have put forward for listing have been critically or in-trinsically flawed. I would rather have seen these estates refurbished and repaired to re-main as council housing for rent to those who need them most, but I am a pragmatist.

I chose my house because it was light, spacious and well designed. There were

Becontree housing estate, Dagenham, London.
opposite: *Lillington Gardens estate, Pimlico, London.*

very few non-local-authority, twentieth-century-designed options around, but it was also cheaper than a privately built property of similar size would have been. I moved from a tiny flat in an Edwardian terrace (which had been illegally converted during the eighties boom, and was smaller than the minimum permitted size), to Parker Morris standards, built-in cupboards and a decent garden, within walking distance of central London. Whilst most of my friends in Victorian houses spent much of their time in knocked-through basement kitchen-diners, sunlight flooded my living room and in summer the garden seemed an immediate extension of it. I like the fact that my neighbours are a mixed lot – some architects and other professionals, who like me have bought on from original Right-to-Buy purchasers, some council tenants and some buy-to-let private tenants. How will this change in the future?

We have reached a crazy position. It seems unlikely that many future Right-to-Buy deals will be struck – property prices have now escalated so that even with the maximum subsidy the cost of purchase would be unaffordable for anyone not earning considerably more than the average wage. Maintaining a few council homes scattered amongst private ones is less cost-effective than maintaining whole estates once was. Councils have an extremely difficult job negotiating the often conflicting demands of leaseholders and their own tenants whenever repair or new services are needed.

Style Council is a celebration of council design, set against this crazy result of circumstance. It will, I suspect, further inflame those who, like James Meek, are angry that 'council houses in London are the new lofts, to be boasted about and refitted with salvaged Bakelite and Formica by the trendiest of their new inhabitants'. He complains that

15

'In addition to all the other indignities the poorest of the poor in London suffer, they now have an extra one: the implication that they never saw the potential.' That is not the message of this book. I hope that it will have wide, positive impact, encouraging councils themselves to carry out much-needed refurbishment and maintenance, and inspiring architects today to learn from their public-sector predecessors, who thought long and hard about how best to provide good-quality housing that would enhance people's lives.

INTRODUCTION

Sarah Thompson

When I first set out to write *Style Council*, I hadn't anticipated – naively, I now realise – how a book based around the private ownership of former council housing would prompt such strong reactions. Having bought and fallen in love with my own ex-council house in 2007, my aim was simply to celebrate the unsung charms of these homes – properties which seemed to me to get a bum rap in terms of their desirability. I also wanted to showcase the creative types who I noticed increasingly were buying them – and not only because they are usually cheaper than the period properties we've all been brought up to covet. I was struck by how the interiors people were creating in these homes were slightly left of field, their owners a little more inclined to do their own thing than follow a pre-ordained path of accepted good taste. Surely this was fertile ground for a very British sort of interiors book?

Yet in my research I met people who were against the idea: they thought a book might bolster what they saw as middle-class gentrification of the ex-council house and the exploitation of cheaper house prices at the expense of those who couldn't get on the ladder at all. Some felt the book would glamorise the controversial Right-to-Buy Act of 1980 – the passing of which, many argue, led to today's chronic housing shortage, but also, fortunately or unfortunately depending on how you look at it, made all the homes in this book available on the open market. Others of an architectural bent thought the book might suggest the council house was a second-rate housing option, and offend the many hundreds of thousands of people who had grown up in post-war council housing. This was a lot to think about, when all I'd really wanted to do was show how a few crazy cats were painting their kitchens in far-out colours.

So it seems that, inadvertently, I have created what must surely be a publishing first – a politically sensitive interiors book. And I feel I need to say here that while the story of social housing in this country is of course a very serious and complex one, *Style Council* isn't so much about the rights and wrongs of it all, as about how everyday people have picked up the baton dropped by Right-to-Buy and run with it, in most cases off the track and into an entirely different race – one full of colour and pattern and vintage furniture and many, many cushions. It is not a book about the property ladder, no house prices are mentioned, there will be no flipping here. And it is not a how-to guide, there are no get-the-look box-outs or styling tips. It is a window on the lives of stylish people living in ex-council homes, an interiors-led temperature check on the way these properties – such an intrinsic part of our domestic heritage – are fettling, thirty-five years since they were first sold off.

It is also a celebration of a seam of British architecture that has been overlooked by the arbiters of taste and style. With Del Boy's flat in Nelson Mandela House for so many years the accepted vision of British council house living, the national consciousness has harboured a less-than-elegant perception of the local authority home. But time marches on, and for a new generation of home-buyers – those for whom the term 'mid-century' is starting to mean almost antique – the modernist lines and brutal concrete facades of the council house are starting to represent a new kind of beautiful. As aesthetics morph and the understanding of what looks good shifts from one generation to the next, the ex-council house is staking its claim in the estate agent's window alongside the red brick Victorian terraces and Edwardian semis with their front porches and garden gates.

Some housing built by local authorities, buildings like Denys Lasdun's Keeling House

(featured on page 75) and Ernö Goldfinger's Trellick Tower in Notting Hill (featured on page 127), have been celebrated for some time. Trellick in particular has enjoyed more than its fifteen minutes of fame, starring in films and being featured on record covers. But for every coffee mug bearing Trellick's instantly recognisable profile, there are a hundred former council homes in streets and lanes across the UK, the architects of which no one will ever know, because they come from an era when the local authority built its own housing and the council architect was just another member of staff. This book is as much a celebration of these homes – and the interiors that people have crafted in these spaces – as it is about their urbane London cousins.

While many interiors books hang their hat on a style or an aesthetic, the homes in *Style Council* share little common visual ground. They are as individual as the architects who designed them. Their owners are from all walks of life, with nothing in common beyond an ability to see beneath the surface and an instinct to upcycle. They share a need to create a home on a budget. And they share an artistic touch – for time and again the people in this book talk of the 'blank canvas' that the square rooms and plumb lines of their ex-council homes afford them. Without imposing period features to respect, they are free to write their own interior rules.

From the flat in Balfron Tower that's a temple to Scandinavian-chic, to a rural nook in Hardy's Dorset packed with tribal artefacts, from the suburban family eco-home in Dublin, to the hipster pad in east London – this book is a celebration of the Great British council home and a tribute to the people who make the positive choice to live in them. They prove that true style knows no boundaries.

The Alexandra and Ainsworth Estate is made of two parallel pedestrian streets, with a 1km-long park running through its middle. There are 520 homes for over 1600 people on the estate.

ARCHITECTS' TONIC

Eleanor Fawcett and Nathan Jones had always imagined they'd settle in east London. They had lived in Clerkenwell for years and in her role as the Head of Design and Physical Regeneration for the Olympic Park, Eleanor felt very rooted in the area. 'That was our patch. So when we heard about this flat, our first thoughts were that it was in the wrong place. North London wasn't really on our radar.'

As architects they knew of the estate – officially the Alexandra and Ainsworth Estate – which was designed by Neave Brown in 1968 for the then Camden Council. It is famous for its distinctive 'ziggurat' or stepped design, which acts as a barrier to noise and vibrations from the nearby railway lines. It's constructed from reinforced concrete and has its own power station, generating hot water and heating for the whole estate. Cars and traffic are restricted to the basement level and all the bright and airy flats open

out onto their own front gardens and the 'streets' and play areas at ground level. With its family-focused ideology and futuristic visual style, the estate, which was completed in 1978, is widely recognised as Brown's finest work. It was Grade II listed in 2003.

Despite their ties to the East End, as soon as the couple came to view it both were converted. 'I can remember whispering to Nathan, "This is amazing,"' recalls Eleanor. Getting the mortgage was tough because all the flats on the estate are constructed of concrete: 'It's a bit of a "computer says no" situation, I think, even though a nuclear war wouldn't damage this place.' With a mortgage eventually secured, they moved in in 2010. 'We were lucky because a lot of the original features were still here: the staircase, the sliding doors. The people before us had obviously been in denial about living in a modern house and there were white shagpile carpets and cornices in every

Structural concrete pillars under the work surface by the window couldn't be moved, so Eleanor and Nathan designed their kitchen as a series of boxes that could be slotted into the spaces between the pillars.

The boxes theme flows right down to the spice rack and CD shelf.

Keeping the bannister and window frames dark is in keeping with Neave Brown's original scheme and cuts through the light that drenches the first-floor kitchen/ dining room.

The bathroom is a masterclass in pared-back simplicity, with fitted cupboards keeping chaos at bay and geometric shapes recalling the estate's original aesthetic.

room. But beyond surface embellishment there isn't much you can do to these places, so it was just a case of stripping it back. It took three years to do – we got married in the middle – but we like to think we've got it back to feeling the way it did originally, laced with some of our own tastes and influences.'

Like all the homes on the estate, the kitchen is on the first floor of the three-storey maisonette. The main living room is above, with a spacious balcony which over-looks their small front garden at street level – Brown's original idea being that parents could keep an eye on their children as they played out in the streets below. 'We use this as a space to come and listen to music and relax, and as a kind of hobby room where I do my sewing. With the balcony it feels like such a big space – it's a real luxury.'

Because the property is listed, they had to work with some of the existing structures

in the kitchen, much of which is at unusual heights and dimensions for standard modern fittings and appliances. 'Some of the original concrete pillars under the work surfaces are actually structural, so we designed our own kitchen as a series of boxes to work around them.'

Nathan drew up the plan and had the wood cut and overlayed with a phenolic-faced resin film, usually used for concrete moulds on building sites. 'One of our neighbours turned out to be an amazing joiner, so he fitted everything for us. I was unsure about having such a dark colour at first but it works with the original scheme – all the windows have dark frames – and it is so bright and sunny in here, we're really happy with how it has turned out.'

The boxes motif runs all the way through the kitchen, from large store cupboards right down to perfectly proportioned spice racks, each box sitting in a kind of relief

Drawers from Ikea were adapted to create a storage wall. Mis-matching the drawer fronts gives a sense of the bespoke.

The headboard puts much-needed space between the bed and the heated walls.

Nina's bedroom at ground level has views onto the
street and the neighbouring Ainsworth Estate.

Having three flights of stairs makes the flat feel spacious and lofty, like a town house.

Originally a bedroom, the first-floor office stacked with books is adjacent to the kitchen and can be easily separated off with the original full-height sliding doors.

against the backdrop. 'We like that it is all clean lines but it's not from a factory – we enjoy all the little details. It's a contemporary take on craftsmanship, with a bespoke edge.'

Off the kitchen they've converted what used to be a bedroom into their home office, with floor-to-ceiling books and a desk overlooking the street. The original, full-height sliding doors mean this room can be easily partitioned off when guests come.

There are more sliding doors downstairs, where a long rectangular space, originally divided into two small children's bedrooms, has been used to create a larger family bathroom and a double room for Eleanor and Nathan. Their architectural skills shine through here – they've created a storage wall between the two rooms based around the carcasses of two Ikea chests of drawers. As Eleanor explains, 'We loved the idea of bespoke cupboards but the drawers are so

expensive to make. So we bought basic drawers from Ikea and fitted them into the wall so that they effectively became the wall. We had the idea of mixing the drawer fronts up and doing a kind of plywood patchwork which makes it look more bespoke.'

They've used more plywood on the bed headboard, which they also had made to their own specifications, ensuring the shelves were just the right size. 'It's nice because it's completely our house. My parents are architects and they designed our family house, so it's been great to be able to do the same with our house.'

The headboard also acts as a buffer between them and the flat's heated walls. All the hot water generated by the estate's own power station is pumped into the walls, which makes it very cosy but also impossible to regulate. 'It was quite an innovation at the time, to embed copper pipes in the concrete. The heating for the whole estate

Light floods into the upstairs living room from the balcony. This is a grown-up space to relax and socialise.

comes on together at the end of October and goes off at the beginning of March.'

The lack of radiators leaves the walls clutter-free, but there is discussion afoot about the long-term viability of the boilers and the copper coils which are coming to the end of their lives. 'It was quite an eco-friendly thing to do in its day,' explains Eleanor, 'but without double glazing it doesn't really tally. It will be interesting to see what happens. We are involved in the Residents' Association, so we are part of the debate.'

They get involved in the community as much as they can, running a weekend scheme for fruit-and-veg boxes in the tenants' hall. Eleanor has also been instrumental in securing funding from the Heritage Lottery Fund to restore the parkland which runs through the middle of the estate. 'It's the first time the HLF has given a grant to a modern landscape, or a park to a housing estate.' The plans include five play areas for children of all ages, as well as new planting. 'It's a bit of a busman's holiday as I'm involved in regenerating the Olympic Park and new playgrounds at work. But it felt like something I was really able to bring. The residents had wanted to do something like that for some time.'

This connection to the wider estate and the issues it faces has been something of a surprise to Eleanor. 'We've never known our neighbours before, but have become drawn very quickly into the community. We really enjoy living here and appreciate the cleverness of the design and how it brings everyone together – as architects we know how hard it is to get that sort of stuff to work. So many residents really appreciate living here and take a great sense of pride in the fact that it's listed – it proves that as an architect you can make a difference to people's lives.'

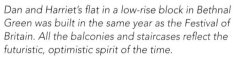

Dan and Harriet's flat in a low-rise block in Bethnal Green was built in the same year as the Festival of Britain. All the balconies and staircases reflect the futuristic, optimistic spirit of the time.

A MAGICAL NOOK

When Harriet and Dan moved into their flat in 2009 the walls were thick with grease and stale cigarette smoke. They later found out that some of their friends had viewed the flat too but decided not to buy it because of the work needed to turn it around.

But the husband-and-wife team, who met while studying fine art at Chelsea College of Art, is hands-on: Harriet is a jewellery designer (the name behind cult brand Tatty Devine), Dan an artist. Together they could see far enough beyond the mess to bag themselves a four-bedroomed apartment just a stone's throw from Victoria Park and the buzz of Bethnal Green – one of the most bohemian parts of the capital. This spacious ground-floor flat, where they live with their daughter Bebe, six, is in a low-rise just one street away from the green lung of the park. The building is part of a cluster of local properties built by the then Bethnal Green Metropolitan Borough Council in 1951 –

some low, some high, all accessorised with cheerful little balconies and interspersed with communal lawns and lolling willow trees. 'We like that it was built in the same year as the Festival of Britain,' says Dan, 'when the country was really showing what it could do. Everything feels so solid and well made.' They looked at a lot of other properties, mostly Victorian, nearby, but were swayed by the cleaner lines of the modern architecture found here. 'It's packed with great little details like the cement skirting boards that don't dent under Bebe's wheels. There's loads of built-in storage and clever borrowed light aspects. This place just felt natural to us.' Dan works from home using the fourth bedroom as his studio. Harriet's studio is in nearby Brick Lane.

The couple approach their decorating style from different angles. Harriet, whose poppy jewellery features laser-cut perspex in bright neon colours, collects objects

Dan, a fine artist, was inspired to paint nasturtiums around the fireplace after a visit to Charleston, the country house in Sussex where members of the Bloomsbury Group met.

The fourth bedroom in Dan and Harriet's flat has become an artist's studio and workshop, where Dan paints and the practical pair keep all their bits and bobs. Jam jars with the lids screwed underneath the shelf are a handy storage solution.

Opening up the hallway made the living room bigger and created space for Bebe's piano.

which are out-of-scale or are made in unexpected materials, like her giant china biscuit from a Parisian market or the enormous Cadbury's Dairy Milk box used as a coffee table. A huge bunch of grapes is draped over the shelves in the kitchen and there's a toothbrush fit for an elephant in the bathroom. Dan – a figurative painter in the traditional sense – prefers natural curios; his studio is cluttered with old skulls, fossils and African carvings, while his guitars and other musical instruments pop up in corners all around the flat. Their mutual style is a medley of contradictions, part down-home and rustic, part dazzlingly modern, always a little bit irreverent and fun.

They love the authenticity and warmth of the Arts and Crafts and Bloomsbury Group styles, a taste reflected in the living-room fireplace and the headboard in their bedroom, both hand painted by Dan. On the walls the naturally muted colours of the

Utility style prevail – tones of faded Bakelite, custard yellows, pale-pine greens and pale greys. But the decoration is by no means safe: the kitchen, where Dan has painted the cupboards in striking black-and-white dazzle patterns inspired by First World War battleships, is a blast of hot mustard yellow. There's more yellow in the bathroom, in which they've installed an original Art Deco bathroom suite (bought on eBay) and jazz-age silver, black and white mosaic tiles. They have 'put back' other period accents where they could, including reclaimed oak doors with porcelain handles and vintage-style light flexes. Modern necessities such as double-glazed UPVC window frames and plastic light fittings have been subtly muted with hard-wearing car paint to give them a patina of age. As Dan says: 'The aim was always to achieve a sense of respect for the building's past, without anchoring it slavishly to an era.' Structurally the couple haven't tinkered with

Dan recreated the dazzle camouflage used on First World War ships when painting the kitchen cupboards. The bold geometric patterns worked by making it hard for the enemy to judge a ship's speed and range.

Tins picked up on their travels – including one from outside a chip shop in Holborn – provide colourful storage in the kitchen. 'We always look for them in Turkish supermarkets but they have to be printed, not film-wrapped, as most are today.'

UPVC window frames have been painted to take the
modern shine off and hung with nostalgic curtains in
yellows and greys.

The flame-orange and yellow headboard was also
inspired by a visit to Charleston, the colours picked
up by Harriet's oriental robe.

the original interior too much. They knocked down a small wall to get rid of a corridor and open up the living room, a move that created enough space for Bebe's piano. And they repositioned the kitchen doorway slightly to maximise the flow of light – and views of the trees – from front to back. 'The building faces east, so we get nice sunny mornings in the kitchen and the warm glow of sunsets in the living room every evening.'

What the sturdy plumb lines, accentuated by streams of light, have given these two artists is a blank canvas. 'We've been able to really put our own stamp on it. It might not have the charm of a period house, but we like that when you come in and close the door, what's inside – and what we look out on – is more important than the building itself. It's a kind of magical nook hidden right here in Bethnal Green.'

Lisa and Jude's cottage garden is laced with tropical palms and Mediterranean vines.

UNCOMMON GARDEN VARIETY

It's hard to believe that Lisa and Jude Murless's home in the Dorset village of West Milton was ever a humble council house. Draped in wisteria, at first glance it has the chocolate-box appeal of a cottage from Jane Austen: a country-cream exterior with roses around the door, green hills and grazing sheep in the distance.

But walk down the sweeping stone steps that lead to the door, and you begin to realise this is no ordinary cottage, or garden. Entwined with the wisteria and lavender are Mediterranean grape vines, olive trees, tropical palms and Japanese maples. Trachycarpus and phormium fill the borders, among which are hidden stone Buddhas and giant fossils. The interior is equally unexpected, with global influences exploding in bursts of hot, earthy colours and dark, tropical woods. It is a place of contrasts and contradictions, where rustic and down-home meets grandiose and ethnic in a family home that is full of personality.

Jude, a horticulturalist, and Lisa, who helps runs the business, have lived here with their three children, India, Theo and Eden, for nine years. The house is one of four clustered in a hamlet set back from a winding country lane, each with a large front and back garden and views across the rolling countryside. They were built by Dorset County Council in the 1950s, but their unusual profile, with distinctive 'cat slide' roofs, where the gable end is lower on one side than the other, gives the buildings a rustic charm reminiscent of a much earlier age.

When Lisa first saw the house – then a three-bedroomed semi-detached with an interior that was 'dated, but in a modern way' – it wasn't love at first sight. 'I'd grown up in service houses and council houses, so for me it was a bit of an issue, buying ex-council. It sounds snobby but I did feel there was a stigma.' Fortunately, Jude was

A side-extension created a dramatic double-height ceiling, tall enough for the abandoned yukka Jude brought home from work one day.

able to persuade her of the potential here. He had grown up in the nearby village of Powerstock and wanted to bring his own family up in the same place. 'We could see there was a structure and a garden big enough for us all, that we could do something with,' says Jude. So they took the plunge and set about transforming it into their unique family home.

With three kids and plenty of animals, the first thing they wanted to do was turn the existing three bedrooms into four. Although the house isn't listed, they had to make sure their plans didn't compromise the roof profile. 'Originally we just wanted to build a second-storey extension out from the side as we only needed an extra bedroom,' says Lisa. 'But the planners said the cat-slide roof was a distinct feature we had to maintain. So we changed our plans and built onto the rear. Looking back, the planners were right – their advice highlighted a lovely feature

that we hadn't really appreciated.'

Building the extension took over a year, much of it without heating or hot water. 'We'd get bored at weekends and knock down walls,' Lisa recalls. It was on such a weekend, while repairing a weak beam, that they 'accidentally' created a vast atrium – a double-height space which they liked so much they decided to keep it. With its giant yukka lolling over the door, it makes an unusually dramatic entrance to the house. 'The supermarket delivery man says it's Gothic,' says Lisa, 'but we can't decide.'

The light and lofty space of the atrium, which also provides a drying-off zone for Jude when he comes home from work covered in mud, is contrasted by the cosiness of the adjoining kitchen, with its dark tiles, log store and wood-burning Rayburn stove which heats all the hot water. Being as self-sufficient as they can be is important to them both. 'I'm a recycling lunatic,' con-

The log-burning Rayburn heats all the hot water – part of their efforts to be as self-sufficient as possible.

fesses Jude. 'I can't bear to see anything being thrown away. So I bring it all home and usually find a place for it somewhere.'

Beyond this is the main living area – big enough for their dining table at one end and a huge wood-burning stove. It's a hard-to-work rectangular room with four doors leading off it – a space they could easily have got wrong. But they've arranged it cleverly, placing the stove and their big comfy sofa at an angle that divides the room neatly into asymmetric zones. The decoration comes from their days spent travelling in Africa and India – warm earthy tones of terracotta and wood, tribal masks, battered leather chairs and sheepskin rugs. 'The blue curtains at the window,' explains Lisa, 'are a reminder of the time we spent in the Canary Islands.'

Also on the ground floor is the office, from which Lisa coordinates their horticulture and landscaping business. She has covered the wall behind her desk in découp-

The supermarket delivery man says the style is Gothic but Lisa isn't sure.

age, using pictures from magazines. There's also a tree trunk by the desk. 'Jude made it for my birthday. It's supposed to be a noticeboard for bills and admin but I keep covering it in pictures of the children.'

Upstairs in the bedrooms, all the beds have been made bespoke from tree trunks cut down by Jude at work. 'We didn't want them to look like they were off the shelf, so we mixed the larch with beech and oak,' says Lisa. Their own bed is a huge double-double. 'It was our way of coping when the kids were small. I fidgeted so much when I was pregnant and then later with feeding the kids in the night, it meant we could all be in the same bed without disturbing each other.'

The back of the house is painted a distinctive marine blue – a further reminder of their time in the Canaries. A huge deck stretches off the back of the living room into the rear garden, providing a convenient log

The tree-house cabin bed in Theo's room was made from wood Jude chopped down in his field. 'A carpenter made sure it was safe and Jude went off with his chainsaw to find all the branches.'

India's attic room is the perfect escape for a little girl and her friends.

store underneath. Jude, who likes to surprise Lisa with unusual, home-made gifts, had an old bath plumbed into the mains water, so she can sit outside on summer evenings while watching the children wash and play.

The whole house is inspired by nature, their travels, the things that matter to them. 'Sure, I would have loved an old manor house that I could renovate,' reflects Jude. 'But here we've been able to create a home based on what we actually wanted, and design a house around the way we live.'

Warren House in Bow is soon to be demolished and the area redeveloped for new housing.

Anish Kapoor's Orbit tower and the Olympic Stadium are part of the view from Fiona's kitchen.

THE FAERIE'S NEST

Lighting and jewellery designer Fiona Gall's professional alter ego is the Emerald Faerie, so it's not surprising her home is a hidden gem. Located on the eighth floor of a gritty-looking high-rise in Bow called Warren House – the last building standing in a soon-to-be-redeveloped 1960s precinct – a trove of treasures glitters behind its bright yellow front door. Originally from south London, Fiona has lived here for five years under a live/work scheme run by the Bow Arts Trust. The scheme sets affordable rents for artists and craftspeople, who in return live as guardians in properties that are up for redevelopment, preventing them from falling into dereliction. Warren House is owned by the social housing landlord Poplar Harca and is gradually being decanted of its original tenants. It will eventually be demolished and the area it occupies regenerated to make way for new housing and public spaces. Fiona's studio is just over the road at

the Bow Arts Trust. She says: 'I moved in on a six-month lease and five years later I'm still here. I'm in a constant state of limbo, not knowing when I'll have to leave, but it's great to have all the other artists around. It feels like I'm part of a proper creative community.'

Fiona's opulent work is inspired by nature in a kind of contemporary take on Art Nouveau. She has extended this to turn her one-bedroom flat into a real-life faerie's nest of gritty glamour, in which vintage and flea-market finds are mixed with the organic shapes and colours of flora and fauna, and the hip style notes of a modern urban woman.

Because she doesn't own the flat, and because she's on a budget, Fiona's home is a masterclass in working with what you've got. The first thing she did when she moved in was give the place a good scrub and paint it white. 'It was pretty dirty and the walls were all purple,' she recalls. The original

A coat made by her friend the designer Reem Alasadi hangs in the hall with some deely-boppers and a sun visor. The bird wallpaper is by another friend, Elli Popp.

black Marmoleum floor tiles are still here, along with some of the reinforced metal-framed windows, the woodchip wallpaper and the standard-issue black-and-white bathroom suite.

Fiona has put her own stamp on things in surprising ways, bringing her style home from the workshop. In the bathroom she has spray-painted over lace onto the cistern and bath panels, creating an ethereal pattern that instantly upgrades the suite. She's hung cut-glass beads from the basin and installed a plastic chandelier picked up at a car boot sale for 50p. 'It doesn't work, I just like the way it looks,' she says. 'I lived in Tel Aviv for a while and that was the one thing from home I took with me. I hung it up and felt like: right, now I can work.'

She chose to make the largest room her bedroom – a decision which means she has a balcony and wakes with the sunrise every morning. 'I figured I spend more time in the bedroom than anywhere else. I'm always trying on outfits and messing around with my clothes.' The floor is littered with her collection of vintage Terry de Havilland shoes and the walls are covered in bespoke wallpapers by her friend Elli Popp. But these aren't expensive indulgences. 'I do a lot of swapping,' she explains. 'I made a chandelier for the Terry de Havilland store, so I swapped it for some of the shoes, and I did the same with jewellery for Elli.'

Also in the bedroom is her 1930s dressing table topped with hand mirrors and perfumes in pretty glass bottles, and her dainty green chaise longue. These ladylike accessories are juxtaposed with the sixties white plastic headboard that once belonged to her parents and the chunky industrial rails on which she hangs her clothes – lace, fur, sequins and wild prints dripping from every hanger. The bed is plump with vintage eiderdowns in shades of chartreuse and eau

The heavy 1970s desk – a gift from her father – takes on a new elegance in Fiona's glamorous living room. The wall above acts as a constantly changing mood board, where she pins her latest inspirations.

Propping up a freestanding fireplace gives Fiona a focal point and a surface for little displays in the living room. Just don't lean on it.

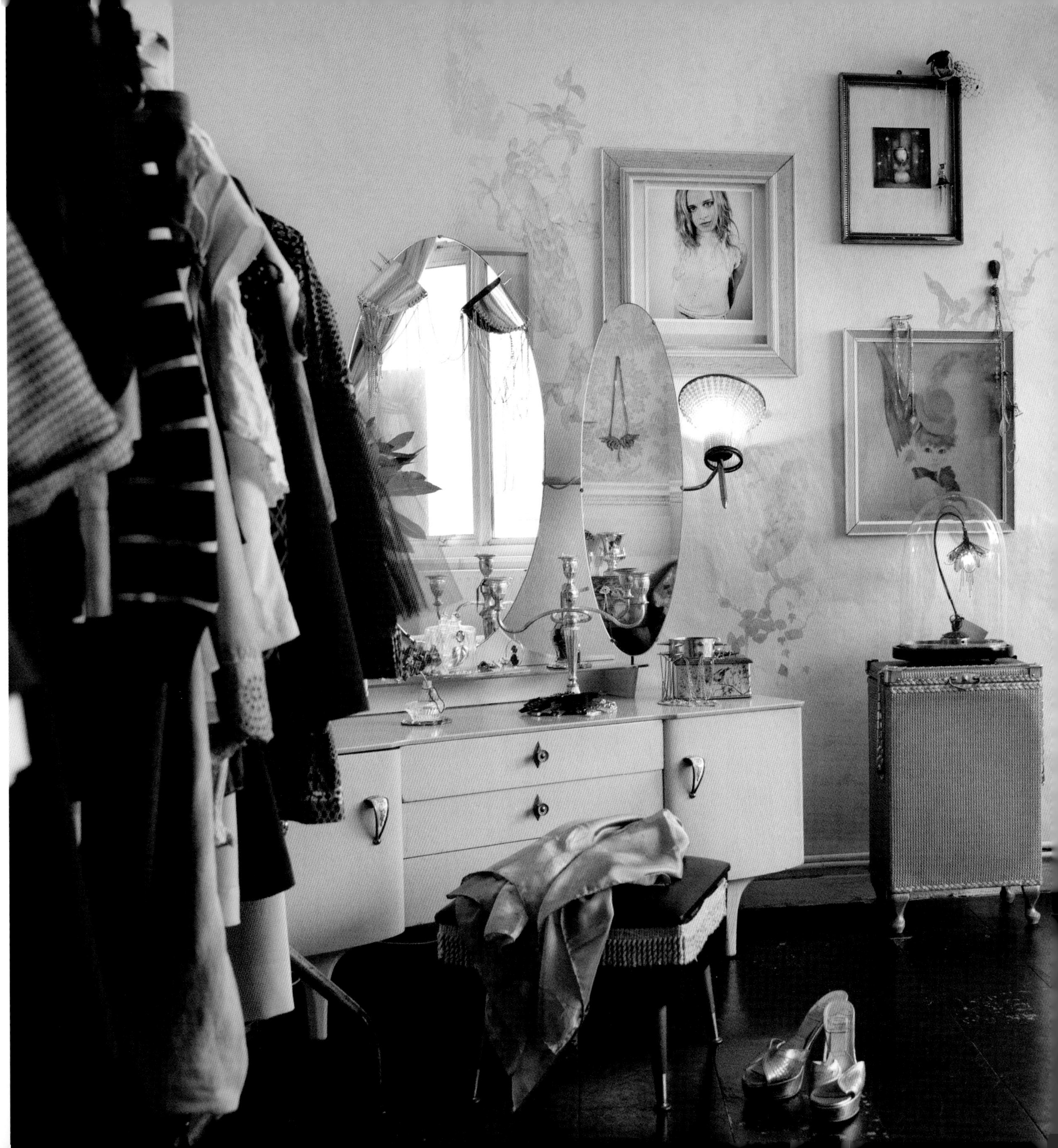

One of Fiona's own creations – a wall lamp dripping with gold and crystal beads – vies for centre stage with a 1930s dressing table in the bedroom.

The wallpaper by her
friend Deborah Bowness
appears mis-hung,
putting a contemporary
twist on the traditional
dado rail.

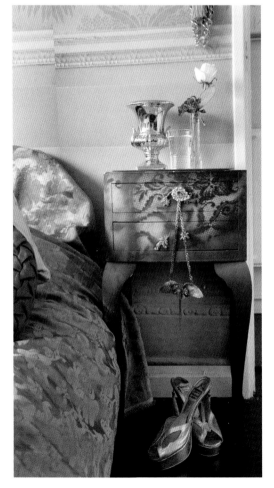

Fiona's collection of vintage Terry de Havilland shoes litters the bedroom floor.

de Nil, but there's a picture of Bob Marley over the headboard. It's part *Great Gatsby*, part *Only Fools and Horses*.

Next door is the office and living space, a smaller room to suit Fiona's faerie-like tastes: 'I don't like working in big spaces.' From here, she has views across to the Olympic Stadium and Anish Kapoor's helter-skelter-like Orbit tower, framed by net curtains at the window and sills edged with the sort of thick gold velvet fringing you might have found on your parents' sofa in the seventies. There's no sofa for Fiona, though; she's plumped instead for dainty chairs in jewel colours, picked up at car boot sales and charity shops. 'Chairs create more of an occasion,' she explains. 'It's more conducive to conversation if I have friends round. If I ever have a sofa it will be one that divides up into single chairs.'

The mantelpiece, topped with vases and trinkets and plants, looks as though it might have belonged to an Edwardian sitting room, but look closely and you realise it's propped casually against the wall and there is no actual fireplace. 'I wanted somewhere to put flowers and display my things, so in the absence of a real fireplace I just made my own.' She's used the same device with empty picture frames around the flat – the familiar markers of a traditional home cleverly turned on their axes. Also in the living room is her desk, made by her father from an old 1970s filing cabinet and desk, and a wall where she pins her creative inspirations in a sort of semi-découpage mood board. It's a small glimpse inside her mind, images of everything from luxury travel to 1950s flooring. Her own work, too, sits on the shelves, sculptural shapes in delicate wire, accented with twinkling lights, butterflies and green bottles. 'It's constantly changing in here. I like moving things around. Sometimes my work will be here and other

Empty frames create a simple focal point above a cabinet and their contents can easily be changed.

Spray-on lace and a length of glass beads around the sink give a shot of insta-glamour to the standard-issue black-and-white bathroom suite.

No-frills white cupboards and tiles are brightened up with colourful pots and pans on display and more glass beading to bring the trademark gritty glamour.

times it won't. I like to keep re-inventing it.'

In the hallway there's more bespoke wallpaper and beside a second fireplace-folly are pegs hung with a madcap selection of coats, hats and sparkly 1980s deely-boppers, which few but Fiona could get away with wearing. The whole flat is fronted by her bright yellow door, with oversized, back-to-front numbers. From the outside it's an explosion of colour and humour on what is an otherwise empty communal landing, where the building's gloomy future feels more real with the faulty lift and the back-in-time staircase. Not every woman would feel comfortable here, but for Fiona it's a much-cherished refuge: 'I always feel really safe here – the building is so secure and there's so much going on outside my window. I like to watch the kids hanging out down in the street and my studio is just across the road. Sometimes I'll head to Tower Hamlets cemetery park, a beautiful

Victorian cemetery full of ivy and vines and rambling woodland. There's so much to inspire my work here. It's a little oasis in the middle of all the fizzy London energy.'

Balfon Tower – Trellick Tower's big brutal sister – is undergoing a major refurbishment.

Lifts serve every third floor, and sit in a separate service tower, joined to the main residential tower by walkways.

BALFRON BEAUTY

When Haidee Drew first moved into her flat in Balfron Tower in the summer of 2014, it had been empty for some time with the windows left open. 'It was pigeon paradise,' she recalls. 'I was scrubbing the floor for days.'

The pigeons clearly didn't appreciate the architectural significance of their temporary accommodation. Balfron Tower is the less well-known but equally beguiling sister of Trellick Tower (featured on pages 127–33), designed by Ernö Goldfinger in 1963 for what was then London County Council and completed in 1967. Widely regarded as a prime example of British brutalism, it shares with Trellick the distinctive service tower, home to all the building's lifts, laundry rooms and rubbish chutes, joined to the main building by eight aerial walkways. It also has passionate fans while others loathe it. Wherever you stand it's a powerful, stop-in-your tracks structure, standing gracefully in its own gardens, with the sounds of the traffic on the nearby A12 cutting through the trees. It has been Grade II listed since 1996.

Balfron is undergoing a complex refurbishment. The social housing landlord Poplar Harca (which also owns Warren House, featured on pages 47–55) is installing new systems to upgrade the building's energy efficiency and bring it into the twenty-first century. The scale of the work, which is being undertaken according to strict conservation rules to protect the general ethos as well as the original features, means moving most of the residents out – or decanting – but as with Warren House, a handful of guardians, mostly affiliated to the Bow Arts scheme for artists and craftspeople, remains to ensure that the building stays alive.

Haidee, a silversmithing graduate of the Royal College of Art, designs and sells contemporary home ware with a nostalgic bent, including mirrors, candelabras and her latest design – a Victorian-inspired acrylic fern pot in the form of Balfron Tower itself. She's also a part-time design technician at a local school.

She had low expectations of life at Balfron: 'I couldn't imagine living in a brutalist tower block. I thought it would be big and grey, like living under a cloud. But after a couple of weeks of being here I couldn't imagine living anywhere else. It's such a sunny place to live.'

Maximising natural light was part of the architect's plan and Haidee's flat, like all the others here, is dual aspect. 'All the bedrooms are on the east side, so I wake up to beautiful morning light streaming in. I take a lot of pictures for my Instagram feed in the morning – I think people get a bit fed up with me.'

Haidee's take on the interiors, which is not overtly 1960s in style – the look is more Scandinavian, with a monochrome palette and natural materials such as wood, leather and metal with the occasional pop of colour – does let light take centre stage. She is also committed to the elimination of unnecessary details and has allowed the structure and form of the space to breathe and be seen – principles of the modern movement of which Goldfinger was a leading light.

This approach is best seen in her kitchen, which, with its private balcony and views across to Canary Wharf, must be one of the best-positioned in London. 'Being on the fifth floor it's the perfect height,' she explains. 'I get all the treetops, so it feels really green, even though the A12 is just next door. And the sunsets you get from here are awesome.' She's painted the floor black and the walls white, and planted the integrated containers on the balcony with shrubs and herbs. 'I'm out here all the time. I always drink my coffee out here in the morning and just come and sit here if I need to clear my head.'

Inside, she's removed most of the 1980s

The original intercom is still working, complete with mini-TV screen.

Books are the colour-pop in the otherwise neutral living room.

An acrylic fern-pot version of Balfron Tower is one of Haidee's latest creations.

The dining table has skyline views above the treetops.
The sycamore benches were a gift from a friend.

From her balcony Haidee can watch the sun rise over Canary Wharf each morning.

The original water tank – not working – is left exposed as an industrial-style nod to the building's heritage.

Scaffolding boards picked up for £1 a metre have been turned into shelves, propped up at one end by an old gas pipe.

fitted cupboards and painted over existing tiles in white to bring them into the monochrome scheme. While pulling out the cupboards she uncovered the old water tank: 'It doesn't work but I like its industrial feel, and that it's part of the building's history. I think it's nice to show functional things, when they are nice. I used the old pipe as a prop for the shelves.'

The shelves – home to tableware and glasses, plants in aluminium pots and glass storage jars – are old scaffolding boards, picked up from a recycling project in Walthamstow for just £1 a metre, sanded and held up by basic brackets.

Haidee loves to cook for friends and entertaining is easy here, thanks to all the space. Not only does she have a good-sized kitchen table (with bench seating fashioned from more scaffolding), but she also has a large dining table in the living room that can easily seat ten. She put it together herself with off-the-shelf legs added to a tabletop used in an exhibition, and the sycamore benches were made by a friend. Set beside floor-to-ceiling windows, this table overlooks the same views as the kitchen. 'I love to cook and the ritual of sharing food with friends, but I think everybody really wants to come here because of the building and the views.'

The rest of the living room is a demonstration in restraint and simplicity, a meticulously planned arrangement that celebrates the space it occupies as much as the items within it. 'I've kind of curated zones in here. So I get a different viewpoint in each corner,' explains Haidee. She's allowed herself small bursts of colour: turquoises and greens from an acrylic fern pot and a print in one corner; yellows and mustards of a rug and a picture by her grandfather in another; lilacs and blues in a screen print by her sister and a piece of framed wrapping paper. There's

Haidee's best-selling range of nostalgic hand mirrors hang on the wall for inspiration.

very little furniture: a simple leather sofa, and some low-level black cupboards discarded from art college. The skeletal stag's head on the wall was a present. She has no television ('I watch films on my laptop') so the focus is instead on her bookshelves – like a large abstract with their bright colours and lines – and the space itself.

Across the hall the bedroom, black and white with a whisper of pale grey, is a further paean to the pared-back. 'I love being under a sloping ceiling – it feels really cosy and safe. It's like living in a ship.' It's a small bedroom but there's ample built-in storage and more of that lovely light. There's not much on display in here – a collection of her wall mirrors (her best-selling products) and a couple of pictures by her sisters, 'all very soft and feminine without being too girly'.

Perhaps the greatest feature, though, and a benefit which few flats can boast, is the one you don't really notice: its dual height. Coming through the front door from the walkway, you immediately descend a staircase and enter the large hall. 'It's an interesting feeling to walk down into the flat. It feels like you've landed, made an entrance. It also makes you feel separate from your neighbours and the walkway – something you need sometimes.' The stairwell also provides a place to hide things – luggage and tools and the mysterious trappings of someone who makes things for a living.

Haidee will have to leave Balfron soon; whether she'll be able to return is unclear but she says that it's exciting to be part of this transitional phase. 'It's weird not knowing how long I'll get to be here, but being here has been such an amazing experience. It has really helped me grow – both personally and as a professional. I'll always treasure it.'

The bed fits snugly under the slope of the emergency staircase. 'It's like being in a ship.'

The Alberta Estate is a mix of flats in tower blocks, maisonettes and residential streets. Catherine speculates that the estate was the brainchild of a Dutch or Flemish émigré architect.

DUTCH MASTER

As director of the Twentieth Century Society – which campaigns for the protection of modern British architecture – Catherine Croft spends her working hours immersed in the clean concrete lines of modern and brutalist buildings. Edifices such as Ernö Goldfinger's Trellick Tower and Balfron Tower (featured on pages 57–65) and the Park Hill estate in Sheffield (pages 83–9) have been preserved for future generations thanks to the society's work.

So it is a surprise to find that her home in south London, which she shares with her ten-year-old daughter Tilda, has dark brick walls, half-hung tiles and a high, slender roof more reminiscent somehow of the iconic windmills of the Suffolk countryside than of an accepted local authority aesthetic.

The house on the Alberta Estate was built in 1958 by the then Lambeth Metropolitan Borough Council. Despite trawling through endless ancient microfiches and council minutes Catherine has been unable to find any more details, but she knows enough to speculate that it was the design of a Flemish or Dutch architect. 'There were a lot of émigré architects working in local-authority departments in the post-war period,' she says, 'so it's not beyond the realms of possibility for the house to have been designed by someone from that region.'

It is the end-of-terrace in a small tucked-away row of houses, each with its own garden and what was originally a pram shed at the front. The wider estate is a mixed development of houses, maisonettes and tower blocks: some with stylish green Festival of Britain-style balconies and staircases; others, like Catherine's, more traditional. All are built in brick with a concrete frame.

What is striking is the sense of seclusion: only a stone's throw from the buzz of Kennington and the main road which thunders into central London, it's so peaceful that it could be in a country village. 'We've always felt very safe here. Tilda has always played outside in the street with her friends. The estate was designed with a sequence of outdoor spaces – front gardens, footpaths and little pocket parks. It's meant that we've always felt very connected with our neighbours.'

Catherine trained as an architect, intending to design social housing. 'But there was no social housing being built by the time I graduated – it was all about splitting bigger houses into flats by that stage.' She was inspired when young by the late-Victorian Arts and Crafts movement which celebrated traditional craftsmanship, natural materials and simple forms, and despite her evident passion for modern-era architecture, there's an undeniable Arts and Crafts spirit about Catherine's home.

This is apparent in the muted palette she has chosen: soft warm pinks, violets and sage greens, all offset by the natural tones of wood. It can also be seen in the collection of pottery all over the house, the shelves of which brim with pieces found in junk shops or made by Catherine herself, contrasting in places with the bright, more modern colours of mid-century glass and ceramics. The textures too reflect it: worn-in wooden flooring (found in a local salvage yard, reputedly from the former County Hall), thick reindeer-skin rugs and soft velvet bedspreads. This is not what you might expect from a modern-architecture devotee, but it fits the tall thin house, which seems to welcome the pared-back, semi-rustic style.

Entering via the original bright blue front door you pass through a small hall and into the main living room. Natural light floods in from the large windows and door at the end, beyond which is a good-sized garden, loosely planted in a country-cottage style. There's a covered terrace at the bottom of the garden where they often eat and where

Large windows provide a canopy of natural light and green foliage from the secluded garden.

A raspberry-pink chimney breast provides the backdrop for a photograph of the Heygate Estate at Elephant & Castle – one of Catherine's many architectural photographs. The estate was demolished in 2014. Catherine and Tilda's guinea pigs sometimes come inside to play in the Ikea doll's house.

Catherine works in the summer: 'I love to look back into the house from this point of view.' When it's colder, she moves the dining table. 'Having the table near the window during the winter, I can at least feel near the garden.'

The living room is a generous size, 'regularly invaded by loads of primary-school kids', and she has kept it simple with neutral shades, plenty of warm wooden surfaces and not much fuss, apart from a bold, raspberry-pink chimney breast and shelves of pottery. In the galley kitchen, the work surfaces are made of a dark hardwood while the fitted cupboards are painted a pretty shade of violet, made bespoke by an interior-architect friend. More open shelves brim with pots and glass and all the quirky little things like tubs of spoons and miniature wooden houses that she has collected over the years.

Going upstairs is a slow process thanks to the hundreds of architectural photographs, etchings and prints hung from floor to ceiling, which demand attention. The first-floor study, originally a bedroom, is painted in tranquil sage greens, and with the dusky light from its high window it seems to lend itself to contemplation. There are sleek fitted cupboards, home to a vast collection of books, and a desk Catherine had made specially high, 'so I can sit on it and see out of the window'. Tilda's room, with the raised bed and cammo netting that befit the urban ten-year-old, is on this floor, as are the original bathroom and separate toilet, also lined with prints and photos of buildings. Catherine hasn't altered the layout 'because it works, and because for family life, you do need discrete rooms'.

Up the second staircase is Catherine's bedroom – her retreat at the top of the castle – the views from which stretch across the estate, past the high-rises with their green

Bespoke fitted cupboards make sleek storage in the kitchen and give breathing space to Catherine's collection of glass and ceramics.

Floor-to-ceiling prints, photographs and paintings make the journey upstairs hard to rush.

A little balcony off the bedroom has room for potted plants and looks over the estate below.

73

The first-floor bedroom has been converted into Catherine's office where more bespoke cupboards keep the room clutter-free. Catherine had the desk made high enough that she could sit on it and see out of the window.

balconies and to the Shard beyond. There's not much room in here for anything more than her fitted wardrobes and bed (its gold and green crewel-work cover speaking again of the Arts and Crafts in its traditional chain-stitched pattern), but looking out from her little balcony, complete with red geraniums, you can see the rhythm of the estate in full flow, the roofs and gardens of her neighbours' homes undulating gently next to one another in a pleasing harmony.

The estate isn't listed, or even a designated conservation area, something which Catherine would like to change. 'It's such a humane and attractive place to live – such care was taken, at all levels, from the overall planning and joinery details, to the amazingly inventive range of building types, and the skilful integration of public spaces. I think recognising it as a conservation area would make us all feel more positive about our surroundings, and a bit more linked to one another as a community.'

For the moment, though, she is just happy to have found her little part of the city: 'I like the feeling that it's so quiet and secluded, but yet so near the centre of London – I can walk to the Embankment in under twenty minutes.'

Or as Tilda puts it: 'I like the way when you walk in it looks like a crowded house, but then you go into the lounge and it's much bigger than you expect. I think that's really awesome.'

Denys Lasdun's Keeling House was the first post-war council housing in the UK to achieve listed status.

COSY KEELING

Mellis Haward studied Denys Lasdun's Keeling House in east London when she was an architecture student at Cambridge. The building, which perches over the Victorian back streets of Bethnal Green like a big white Stickle Brick, was the first post-war council housing in the UK to be recognised as architecturally significant, and was Grade II listed in 1993. Lasdun's vision was for a more humane type of modernism; he felt that the rigid principles of some modernist housing failed to encourage a convivial neighbourly spirit. He designed Keeling House with four wings, like a butterfly, with the front doors all looking onto each other: the idea being to create everyday contact among residents, as experienced by the people living in the streets below. Each dwelling is a two-storey maisonette with its own front door; there's a central lift tower and what was once a communal drying area that everyone has to pass through. This ap-

proach was revolutionary, and although there were issues over its construction, Keeling House continues to be regarded by many as a beacon of modernist social housing.

Mellis had never considered that she might one day find herself living here. 'I was looking for my first place to buy and kept seeing these Victorian conversions – but they were always disappointing. Then I came to a party here in Keeling House and remember thinking it just felt so refreshing. The views were beautiful and it felt so peaceful. I got home and searched online to see if any flats were available and this one had just come on the market. It was all done by the following week. It felt really fated.'

Her flat – located on the eighth and ninth floors – had a few dodgy pink walls: 'There was a bit of glitter paint I had to get rid of and some vinyl floor tiles I pulled up,' she recalls. But there wasn't much else to do

Mellis and Kevin found they shared a love of
mid-century style, and Mellis was very pleased
to welcome Kevin's Ladderax shelving unit and
Robin Day sofa to the mix.

Mellis found a book about housing in the 1960s, with a picture of Keeling House on the front, at a car boot sale.

beyond the cosmetic. 'The fabric of the building is so solid – it's just thick concrete – there's very little you can do to the space unless you want to get really invasive.'

Besides which, she points out, the layout is already as well thought out as possible. 'I like what a neat plan it is – that appeals to me as an architect. There is no waste of space – very little circulation area, no long corridors or big empty landings. There are built-in cupboards. Every bit of space is useful, particularly the balcony – it's so important if you are living in a high-rise to have some outside space. And although all the front doors look on to each other, all the balconies face outwards, so it always feels very private sitting out there. It's very clever.'

The uninsulated concrete construction can make the flat feel a little cold at times, so Mellis's aim inside has been to create cosiness and warmth. She says: 'It would be tempting, given the building's slightly James Bond exterior, to go all leather sofas and white walls. I wanted to work with it and be complementary to its era, but at the same time create something really snug and homely.'

One way she has achieved this is by making her own furniture. Using cheap and cheerful plywood and pieces of reclaimed timber, she has created a few key items that fit snugly into their space and bring an authentic, homely feel to the flat. 'As an architect I'm used to making models and joining wood. I don't like to buy new things if I don't have to, so I built the floating shelves above the sofa. I wanted lots of books around but I don't like the heavy feeling of floor-standing shelves and how much space they take up. The desk in the office is an old door given to me by my parents. I gave it some legs from Ikea and it fits perfectly in the recess. I also made my own dressing table – it has little compartments for my make-up and jewellery and the alarm clock, and I covered the

plywood in pink fibreglass to give it more rounded edges. Making your own furniture is a real labour of love but it's pretty satisfying.'

Other pieces of furniture are worn-in second-hand or family items handed down, such as the wardrobe in her bedroom that belonged to her grandmother and the Scandinavian dining chairs around her Ercol table in the kitchen/dining area: 'I love my chairs, they're from my grandpa. He bought them in Scandinavia in the 1950s. He was an architect too.'

Mellis's parents are also both architects and it was her father who bought her a hammer drill when she moved into Keeling House. 'He taught me how to use it properly, with Rawlplugs. It goes in like butter – it's so satisfying when you are used to using a normal drill.'

But it was to lead to something even more rewarding. After drilling holes in her walls quite late at night not long after she had moved in, she received a letter from her downstairs neighbour, Kevin, politely complaining about the noise. She went downstairs to apologise and a few months later the pair were an item. When the contract came to an end on Kevin's rented flat, he moved upstairs to Mellis's and they've lived there together ever since.

Fortunately, as a graphic designer Kevin shares much of her visual taste. 'We both love the 1950s colour palette,' says Mellis. 'When he moved in we took a swatch of Le Corbusier's wallpapers to the DIY shop and colour-matched the green in the kitchen and the blue on the stairs. I also loved quite a few of Kev's things, like the Robin Day sofa and the Ladderax shelves in our living room. We did have a tense picture situation at one point. We didn't have enough room for them all, so we had to pick our favourites of each other's. We've since bought a few

*Being on two floors makes the flat feel like a house.
A painting by Mellis's dad hangs over the stairs.*

In the office, Mellis made her own desk using an old door and painted some basic shelf brackets yellow, so they stood out against the flint-grey wall.

The look is simple in the bedroom, where the dressing table Mellis made for herself sits beneath the window.

things together, like the film poster we picked up in India.'

That she should meet her partner here is for Mellis just part of the power of Keeling House. 'I remember when I came to view the flat there were people chatting in the foyer and I thought what a warm and friendly place it seemed and hoped that I might also be able to live here and be part of it. That dream has become a reality, not only with meeting Kev but with everyone here. We have a Keeling House email group where we discuss issues and share ideas, and we always get together for Christmas drinks. Some friends questioned why I was moving into this cold council house, so it has been exciting for me to bring my vision of a comfy, cosy home here in Keeling House to life.'

The Park Hill estate is undergoing a transformation in the hands of developer Urban Splash.

PARK HILL LIFE

James and Emma Mills were living in a back-to-back terraced house in Huddersfield when they heard that the flats at Park Hill in Sheffield were coming on the market. 'We saw it advertised and we knew then there was no other option. It was a case of we buy one of these or we don't buy anywhere,' says James.

The pair had met in Leeds but wanted to move to Sheffield as James was working there. 'The house in Huddersfield was lovely, but it wasn't us. We are very much city people and we wanted that urban feel. It's the height that's appealing – we like that we can see everything. Houses at street level feel so inward-facing. Sheffield is a valley, so from up here you feel like you are on top of the world.' Looking out from their office window, with the very tallest of the city's street lights below eye level, it's easy to see what he means.

The controversial estate, completed in 1961 and designed by architects Jack Lynn and Ivor Smith in 1957, was inspired by Le Corbusier's famous Unité d'Habitation, with a 'deck access' or 'streets in the sky' scheme rather like a cruise liner. Its flats rise some fourteen storeys high, looming over the city as it tumbles down into the valley below. Although originally the curtain walls of Park Hill were in bright yellows and oranges and reds, over the years they faded back to the original concrete. Like many of its brutalist siblings across the country, the estate has attracted plenty of criticism from those who dislike its uncompromising profile, but despite its detractors it was Grade II listed in 1998, making it Europe's largest listed building.

In the 1970s and '80s Park Hill went through hard times and garnered a reputation, like so many estates, for crime and urban decay. But in 2011 it was taken over in a part-privatisation scheme by the developer Urban Splash in association with English

84

Park Hill's 'streets in the sky' were made wide enough for a milk float, although none have visited recently.

James and Emma have covered a wall in clippings from their favourite manga cartoons.

Heritage; the buildings are gradually being restored and the flats turned into a very modern mix of private homes, businesses and social housing. A major feature is the return of the distinctively colourful curtain walls.

James and Emma were among the first to put a deposit down on a private apartment at the new development in 2013. 'I knew about Park Hill's architectural background but never imagined I could actually live here,' says James. 'We knew it had seen better days but with it being an Urban Splash project we also knew it was going to be special. Working in the field, we come across a lot of interesting places but this was the place for us, even if it meant we'd have to sleep on the floor.'

Thankfully things didn't get that bad; the couple, who were married in 2012, inherited some money from a relative, enabling them to deck out their flat just the way they wanted. With almost a year between putting the deposit down and moving in, they had plenty of time to plan everything in detail.

'We both use CAD [Computer Aided Design] in our work, so we did endless CAD designs on our computer from home in Huddersfield. Even just choosing the sofa took for ever. We wanted furniture that would match the building so we modelled things up constantly so we could get an idea of how it would look. We fell out quite a lot as we both have quite strong opinions and we both like bold things. Neither of us is half anything.'

The flat came with the simple white kitchen already fitted, and the distinctive exposed concrete walls, complete with holes from the original light fittings. 'I think our parents weren't keen on the concrete wall but have come round to it. Most people seem to enjoy it because it's so different.'

With the blank canvas in place, they went

The kitchen came pre-fitted with the flat. Emma says James has discovered a new tidy streak thanks to its sleek lines.

James and Emma have front-row seats to the daily transformation of the estate from their dining table.

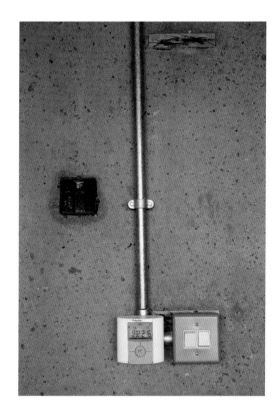

Concrete walls, complete with original electrical cavities, have been left exposed.

full throttle with a bold, colourful look which they feel reflects their personality as a couple, including a zingy lime-green feature wall and aubergine leather sofa that take centre stage in the living room: 'We felt like we could really go wild here,' says Emma, 'in a way that we never could before. There are bold colours on the outside of the building, and we really enjoy the strong edges, so we wanted to reflect that internally. We both hate pastel colours.'

They share a love of all things Japanese and spent their honeymoon in Japan: they have decorated the internal doors upstairs in clippings from manga cartoons. 'It took three or four months in the end,' says James. 'The pictures get racier nearer the bedroom, and are more palatable near the living-room end. I became so engrossed in it I began to build storylines into it.' Emma keeps her collection of manga figures in the bedroom, which they use as an office-cum-gaming

*Bold, bright colours inside complement the primary
colours of the distinctive curtain walls of the exterior.*

Colour-pop Ikea light fittings on the stairs continue the motif of bright, impactful colour against concrete.

room. 'Everyone assumes they're James's,' she says, 'but I've been in love with Japan ever since I used to play Final Fantasy with my younger brother. My whole family loves Japan.'

Sitting in the main living room with its pristine surfaces ('we like to keep everything clean and tidy and organised') and floor-to-ceiling windows, you could easily imagine yourself in a Tokyo skyscraper. 'We sit and eat at the window every evening,' says James. 'We rarely close the curtains. Emma describes this as our holiday home. It's a different lifestyle. We're happier because of the environment we live in. And we both feel more creative.' It's surprisingly quiet, too. 'The only noise we hear is the buses shifting down a gear as they go up the hill sometimes. We're of the opinion that if you don't want any noise you probably shouldn't live in the city.'

Because the redevelopment is ongoing,

There are only two curtains in the flat: one in the shower and the other they had made for the bedroom 'to make the room dark, not because anyone could ever see in'.

they feel they've yet to truly access the benefits that living on the communal 'streets in the sky' will bring. 'We're only the first flank to be redeveloped,' says James. 'We go to community meetings every couple of months and it's nice to see everybody and hear about what's going on. There's an interesting mix of young people in social housing, and older people who have bought their flats. Generally nothing much happens, but people get to share ideas and set things up.'

Originally they imagined they might stay at Park Hill for a couple of years but have found they are reluctant to think about moving on. 'Being here caters for everything we need. We're five minutes from the train station and five minutes' walk into town. The convenience of being here is very beneficial.'

Two 'ex-corpo' houses at the opposite ends of the same street in Dublin have been given space-enhancing extensions.

DUBLIN DOUBLE

A TALE OF TWO EXTENSIONS

At opposite ends of the same street in Dublin 8 sit two very different ex-council houses: one a busy family home, the other a just-so bachelor pad. Though different in their interior styles, both have been cleverly extended by the same architect and show how Dubliners are adapting the ex-corporation house to suit twenty-first-century life.

Built in the 1920s by Dublin Corporation as affordable homes for factory workers, they're in an area referred to by the locals as 'the Tenters', apparently because linen used to be dried here on tenterhooks. More recently, since the Celtic Tiger (the name given to the economic growth and subsequent crash that hit Dublin between 1995 and 2000), the area has become popular with middle-income families no longer able to afford more desirable parts of the city. (Such

is now the level of gentrification that it's also sometimes referred to by true locals as 'the lavender-belt', or 'the muesli-belt'.)

Architect Jim Lawler, whose firm Melted Snow designed extensions for both these houses, explains: 'Houses in the Tenters don't have period-house styling, but ten years ago were an affordable option for young urban professionals and families who wanted to stay in the city and didn't want to be suburban. With budgets being tight post-Celtic Tiger, they represented a good deal in terms of what could be achieved.'

And as with every ex-council home featured in this book, their simple, fuss-free lines meant that for those daring enough to think outside the box, there were interesting things to be done: 'It was a case of gutting the floor plan and starting again with a front and a back. They were a blank canvas.'

The Irish-cedar box extension gave Catherine and family plenty of room for a log store and bike shelter at the front of the house.

THE FAMILY ECO-HOME

Catherine Cleary's house in the Tenters wasn't pretty when she and her family took it on. Pebbledashed, with UPVC doors, poky rooms and an ugly brown garage, it wasn't the house she'd imagined ending up in. 'My parents were a bit surprised. I think they saw it as taking a step backwards,' she recalls. But like many of Dublin's urban professionals – Catherine and her husband Liam are both journalists – they'd felt the financial wrath of the changing economy. The reasonable asking price and end-of-terrace location of this 'ex-corpo', with its three bedrooms and small back garden, gave it the potential to be a comfortable family home for the couple and their three young sons.

From the outset their vision was green. 'We knew we wanted to do an eco-build,' says Catherine. 'Liam was an eco-correspondent at the time and had worked for the environment minister so we were keen to future-proof ourselves in terms of energy costs and efficiency. We wanted to create a comfortable, cosy family home and at the same time not be spending all our earnings on energy.'

Unusually for the time (this was 2007, before the notion of eco-building had entered the national consciousness) they employed an energy consultant, who tested the building for airtightness and suggested ways they could improve its fabric. They installed a water-harvesting tank in the garden so that all their grey water (radiators, toilets etc.) would be free indefinitely, and wrapped the house in external insulation to keep heating costs down.

'They were expensive things to do at the time – the water tank especially felt like we were just burying money in the garden, but

The front room, with its original fireplace, is a cosy space where the kids play and practise piano.

The sleek white kitchen merges seamlessly into the main living space.

Japanese-style sliding doors can close off the playroom when required.

The extension doubled the size of the main room, where the kids tear up and down, in and out of the garden.

Catherine had a 1930s bath – picked up on Freecycle – re-enamelled rather than buy a new suite.

The extension tapers to a window where Catherine works with views overlooking the city.

water rates have just come in here in Ireland so we've really started to see the cost bene-fits. The foam insulation on the outside has made the house about three inches fatter all over – it's like we've wrapped it in a giant Puffa jacket. It's so cosy, and never draughty. If we lived in a Victorian or Georgian proper-ty we might not have been able to do that – there are lots more restrictions on older houses.'

They might not have been able to build their incredible extension either, had they been restricted by period features. This sleek, contemporary addition, clad in Irish cedar, hugs the back of the house, creating a huge kitchen/dining room with windows onto the garden, and a generous bike store at the side for logs and the many wheeled vehicles that come with family life. It also gives them a shower room and utility room on the ground floor, plus an extra bedroom and a large landing upstairs with desk space

and views across the city. This simple addi-tion to the original structure is quite daring at the same time: a cedar-clad spaceship that landed here one day and decided to stay.

Internally, their home style reflects their green ethos with eco-paints in earthy tones, reclaimed flooring and industrial-style lighting. They reused much of the existing sanitary ware and tried to work with the house's early-twentieth-century feel. 'We picked up a 1930s bath on Freecycle and had it re-enamelled, which probably cost more than it would have to buy a new suite but it felt right.'

They've hung sliding doors between the front living room – part of the original house, where the kids watch TV and play with their toys – and the main kitchen/dining room, so the two can be separated when needs be. With its comfy armchairs, big dining table, open-plan kitchen and wood-burning stove,

Eco-paints in natural shades, wooden floorboards and simple light fittings make the place feel relaxed and unpretentious.

the kitchen/diner is the heart of the house. There is space enough for the kids to roar around and the grown-ups to kick back, and it is filled with natural light from the floor-to-ceiling windows onto the back garden. It's hard to imagine how they'd find a room so perfectly adjusted to their family life anywhere else.

'I do still occasionally get Victorian-house envy,' says Catherine, 'but recently we've seen lots of new families move into the area. The kids love hanging out in the park and we have great neighbours here. It's really vibrant. I can't see us being so comfortable anywhere else.'

The teak-clad extension leads onto a decked patio garden with palm trees and bamboo, designed for zero maintenance.

THE BACHELOR PAD

Buying a house in the Tenters felt completely natural to Pete Reddy.

'I was born around the corner, my best friend lives opposite. As soon as I walked through the door I knew it was the right house. I didn't even want to look upstairs.'

Pete, a graphic designer, had always been interested in architecture: 'I knew I wanted to do something progressive, a little bit extreme – not just a boring conservatory. Living on my own, I also knew I didn't need an extra bedroom, so the extension could really be about the way I lived.'

His solution was a two-storey addition to the side, which although it ate into the small garden, gave Pete a new dining room downstairs and a spacious upstairs bathroom. It also created a large landing with a light well – a huge rectangular window in a teak frame,

made of opaque, bulletproof glass. 'It's like a Japanese paper theatre when the light shines through it at night – you get all these patterns from the plants in the garden.'

Externally the box is clad in teak strips, making it look ultra-modern but also timeless, thanks to the natural wood. From the dining room the floor-to-ceiling glass doors open onto the back garden, which with its decking, palm trees and ground cover of pebbles and chippings is a natural extension of the extension. 'The garden is informed by low maintenance. Palms have enough height so I'm not overlooked. With evergreen bamboo there's no shedding. I just wanted to simplify everything for myself. But I was also into natural – I didn't want anything plastic or cheap looking.'

Inside, Pete's style mixes his love for natural, organic materials and textures with a solid, masculine feel. The dining table in white oak, though Swedish, hints at a

The backlit artwork in sheet metal changes naturally over time.

Japanese aesthetic, with high-backed chairs and rigid lines. The hues are neutral and there are more plants: cactuses and succulents with bold, graphic shapes. 'I don't know what half of them are but I like having plants around. I don't really like trinkets. I have an attic full of vases and candlesticks that people have given me.'

Wherever you stand in the living area, your eye is drawn to the dining-room centrepiece, a large metal rectangle backlit by tube lighting. It's a bespoke artwork, devised by Pete and architect Jim Lawler to bring more light to the space and extend the idea of living with nature. Pete explains: 'We bought a piece of sheet metal and asked them to cut it in the proportions of the golden section [a ratio thought to have been devised by the ancient Greeks, used by artists for centuries to achieve aesthetically pleasing proportions]. I left it untreated, so it's changing all the time and getting more and more interesting as the years go by.'

Upstairs, the extension has given Pete an indulgently large bathroom. 'I loved the idea of having it really plain.' The walls are clad in sheets of flinty grey roof slating. 'I like how it feels tiled but it isn't. I wanted the bathroom to feel like it was kind of tough and would really stand up to things.' To keep the space uncluttered, he built the shower behind a storage wall that also acts as a cupboard for all his towels and products. The skylight over the shower bathes it in its own pool of natural light. The rest of the lighting in here is deliberately low-level, making the transition into the landing with its large, screen-like light well and jungle-green walls all the more elevating.

Across the landing there's a small office and Pete's bedroom, once a much smaller room with the original bathroom off it. 'It was all a bit poky upstairs so I got rid of all the doors and opened up all the space. I just

The extension gave Pete the chance to indulge in a large bathroom. The room is clad in sheets of tough roof slating.

wanted to open everything up. I don't even have any curtains.'

This is a home built around the way Pete lives, to his own specifications, modern and directional, yet still very much within the context in which he grew up. 'I love it here. I like the scale of it and the peacefulness of the street but being so near the city. I'm not planning to move. I'm a city boy and I feel happy here.'

The light well on the landing is made from opaque, bulletproof glass. At night shadows from the palms outside create patterns on the glass.

Cuff Point has a jammy location on Columbia Road, a stone's throw from the fun and games of Shoreditch – one of London's liveliest areas – and the bustling weekend flower market. The views from Jane's flat stretch from Greenwich to Alexandra Palace.

| Cuff Point, London | Architect: Unknown
Council: Tower Hamlets London Borough Council | 1971 |

POINT OF VIEW

It is probably nothing more than a happy co-incidence that a costume designer should come to live in a building called Cuff Point, but it's hard not to feel a sense of destiny being fulfilled at Jane Petrie's flat in Columbia Road, so perfect is the fit.

Jane's flat is on the top floor of the brown and blocky 1971 high-rise – not quite blocky enough to be brutal, but with determinedly brutal aspirations – at the Shoreditch end of the Newling Estate, now one of London's most desirable addresses. She shares it with her partner Trevor, who also works in film, and their five-year-old son Dougal.

Jane bought the flat in 2000 with a friend (whom she and Trevor have since bought out). She remembers how hard it was to manage. 'The place was changing but you still had all the old veneer and wood yards up Hackney Road. There were very few shops and you could never find a cash point. Agents and surveyors didn't understand the

area yet and it was really hard to get a mort-gage, especially on a high-rise.'

Because she was young, Jane knew she didn't want to buy anywhere that felt old-fashioned or too much like a family home. 'I felt uneasy about buying ex-council – I objected to them being sold off – but it was kind of our only option in the area. It was what we could afford. And I knew I wanted somewhere modern, with square edges and plenty of light.'

The light she has ended up with is almost celestial, and the views are panoramic, stretching on a clear day from the Dome in Greenwich all the way to Alexandra Palace. The flat is arranged on a simple L-shape and whether it's because of what she does for a living – Jane has designed costumes for such films as *Notting Hill*, *28 Days Later*, *Moon* and *Suffragette* – or just because of who she is, she has made it into a home that fills every space and is also incredibly

As a costume designer working on films, Jane often picks up interesting things from sets. She found this Danish fold-away-office while working on the film Broken. 'My whole life is in there.'

The Ercol bed-settee, and the old school desk masquerading as a coffee table, epitomise Jane's clever approach to space-saving.

Jane knocked the hatch through from the kitchen into the living room. 'I called my dad, who is an architect, afterwards, to check it was OK. He said you can knock a much bigger hole in the wall than you think before it falls down!'

Jane's friend Rocky made her kitchen doors from old tea chests and fruit crates. 'It was a collaboration really, we picked up the crates down at the market.'

comfortable to move around. The surface elements and the overall look – a fun, sixties- and seventies-inspired vibe ('We didn't want to go any earlier, we wanted to work with the bones of the building') – are almost secondary to what has been achieved in terms of making a small space work as a family home.

Jane has left the floor plan alone, apart from turning the bathroom back into a separate toilet and bathroom: a move that goes against the modern zeal for knocking through, but which has given them more storage space (and proves that sometimes the original designs are the best). So that people can still wash their hands in the smallest room, Jane has fitted a toilet from Japan that combines a basin with the cistern, using the waste water from the basin for the flush. The walls in the toilet are hung with bits and pieces from film sets she's worked on, particularly old wooden rulers –

a reminder of her knack with size and fit.

What was the largest bedroom has been divided into two by a clever storage wall. On the far side – through an old railway-carriage door also from a film set – is Dougal's bedroom: a little boy's haven with pirate bed, rope ladder and bird's-eye views across the ocean of London.

On the near side of the same wall is the family workshop. Here Trevor keeps his tools and DJ decks (on surfaces built to his specifications because, at six foot two, he struggles with conventional bench heights) alongside Dougal's craft activities and Jane's boxes of buttons and thread. The room is lined in shiplap timber – a reminder of Jane's childhood. 'We had a room clad in shiplap when I was growing up,' she says. 'I like how warm it feels.'

The warmth of wood is a recurring motif that gives the flat a homely, worn-in feel. 'I like how you can use all sorts of woods

Cladding the walls of the hobby room in shiplap timber, Jane wanted to recall the cosiness of the bathroom in her parents' house in the 1970s.

together and they never clash. I find myself overwhelmed by choice with colour and paint. You know where you are with wood.'

The kitchen cupboards (also built slightly higher for Trevor, the main cook) are made from old tea chests. The look in here is semi-industrial, with few frills apart from the bright colours on the side of a fruit crate or an old milk bottle. Pared-back lines hide the functionality of the room: a concealed door in the work surface for access to the top-loading washing machine; finger holes instead of handles; the toaster hiding snugly in a recess. It feels at the apex of modernity but with the red Marmoleum floor and the hatch through to the lounge, recalls its seventies roots. The hatch, with the kitchen table beneath, links the two main rooms and borrows light from the living room, which has floor-to-ceiling windows and a plant-filled balcony. Everything works hard to save space: the bed-settee; the coffee table

made from an old school desk which doubles as a magazine store.

The living room is also Jane's work space: what looks like a straightforward sideboard reveals itself as a fully functioning home office. Another great find from a film set, this simple piece of furniture encapsulates Jane's home ethos: neat and functional, but in keeping with the era of the building and with understated good looks. 'This is our favourite room,' she says. 'We often just sit here in the evening with the door to the balcony open and listen to the sounds of the city.'

But the feel-good factor of Jane's flat isn't just about what's behind the front door. To live here at the top of this vertical street is to be part of a unique community, with many other families around them. Being on the top floor, the flat is serviced by both lifts, unlike the flats below; something which Jane says puts Dougal at an advantage on

Jane saw a toilet with a sink in the cistern while travelling in Japan and managed to track one down in a bathroom shop in Brixton. 'The one in Japan had a lot more whistles and bells but I knew there must be something similar in the UK.'

birthdays and at Christmas, as he receives cards and gifts from almost everyone in the block. Trevor and a few of the other residents even run a little gardening club, tending green areas at the foot of the building. 'We joke about it, but it's kind of like the Bauhaus dream.'

For Jane, though, who is originally from Fife, it will always come back to the views. 'Trevor and I both grew up by the coast,' she explains. 'We sometimes say living here is a bit like being by the sea, with all the space and openness. We don't have a lot of space inside but it's what we look out onto that's magical.'

*A useful shelter for
the bins at the front
symbolises the kind soul
of her ex-council house
to Christabel: 'It was
built to look after you.'*

ART HOUSE

When Christabel Stewart and Darren Flook moved into their 1979 ex-council house in Hackney, they threw out, among many other things, thirteen mattresses and a burnt-out fridge full of cockroaches.

'There were two beds in every room and mortice locks on every door,' recalls Christabel. 'The house had obviously been let by-the-bed to people working as kitchen porters. We found hundreds of clocking-in tickets for a big restaurant nearby. We had to have the whole house steam-cleaned.'

Despite its vagabond appearance, the couple couldn't resist the allure of the three-storey town house, just a short walk from London Fields and the vibrant scene that was starting to emerge in Hackney. As Christabel explains: 'We'd been living in Bethnal Green in a flat with no heating and really wanted to move as we had our son Ludo by then. We'd been looking at all sorts of places but when we saw this we knew instantly what an amazing family home it would make. It was a bit grotty, but it seemed so exciting to us that we could have a front door and a back door. And there was so much cupboard space. I thought only posh people had so much cupboard space.'

When they moved in they knew they wanted simply to clear everything out and paint it white. They both work in contemporary art and together ran a gallery called Hotel in Bethnal Green for ten years. Darren continues to work as a gallerist and Christabel is now a freelance curator and lecturer in fine art at Kingston University. 'Coming from galleries, we are used to dealing with white boxes. It's where we feel comfortable,' explains Darren.

The kitchen was in such a bad way – there were other clapped-out appliances as well as a healthy commune of cockroaches – that it was the one room they knew they had to do up, even though they were on a budget.

Much of the Scandinavian furniture they owned already but it seemed to be more at home in this setting.

The print of Le Corbusier's Modulor Man was a gift from an art dealer friend.

'We did it all really simply. The units are from Ikea and the work surface is reclaimed school-science benches.' Christabel's collection of vintage Picquot Ware teapots, inherited from her grandmother, takes pride of place on the open shelves along with an anglepoise lamp and an old classroom-style clock. 'The kitchen table Darren picked up at an art fair.'

They have resisted the temptation to call in the architects and 'open up' the space downstairs, choosing instead to keep the small room at the front of the house as a play space for Ludo, which means he can be doing his thing while the grown-ups are in the kitchen at the back. With its door onto the garden, this is where they spend most of their family time.

'We are very into food and entertaining so we can be putting the world to rights around the kitchen table while Ludo and his friends are tearing around,' says Darren.

This respect for the bones of the building extends right through their home, as Christabel explains. 'We kept the reinforced glass in the kitchen door because we quite liked it and we've got all the original aluminium door handles. Darren wanted to take off the skirting boards but I am a bit obsessive about keeping the original things so they stayed.'

They've stripped the floors back to plywood sheets in some rooms and in others have given them a simple lick of paint. 'Our job has mostly been taking off layers that other people have added – making sure we could see to the edges of the room. We haven't added anything. The whole place felt a lot smaller when we moved in. We like seeing underneath things – it makes it feel much better.'

They already owned much of the mid-century furniture, including a G-plan glass-topped coffee table, a teak sideboard

The birdcage is home to a white budgie called Birdie, found in the street and rescued by Christabel and son Ludo one day. Plants from Columbia Road market soften the edges of the room.

and Danish leather sofas, which took on a new lease of life on arrival in their first-floor living room. 'It all felt really natural, like it was meant to be here.'

It's true that the warm, worn-in hues do seem to fit this room, where the huge sash windows, complete with original wooden safety bars, let sunlight flood in. 'It's quite nice to have the view over the street. The area has become so vibrant and there's a real mix of residential and shops. The Violet Café is just at the end of the road and we're near Ludo's school. We feel a real sense of engagement with the area.'

The only real embellishments are some pretty impressive plants, picked up at the nearby Columbia Road flower market. 'Plants are really important to me,' says Christabel. 'If you're trying to keep things simple and plain, they soften everything. If you look at some of the original modernist houses, they are full of plants. They just look right in these situations.'

The other diversion is art. 'If you have a successful fair you invest in something,' says Darren. 'So in that sense our pieces tell our story, what we are interested in at any time.' They have work by many leading contemporary artists, including Amy Yao and Duncan Campbell, but for Christabel perhaps the most treasured piece is a print of Le Corbusier's Modulor Man. The iconic image of a man with his arm raised represents an anthropometric scale of proportions which the Swiss architect devised to make his own buildings – his machines for living in – perfectly fit the human form. The print was given to Christabel by a friend who was threatening to throw it out and it now occupies pride of place in their downstairs hall.

As the house extends over three floors, they have had to acclimatise to their own private sense of scale and proportion. 'Vertical living is something you have to get used to,' says Darren. 'The house is

Utility-style Picquot Wear tea and coffee pots were inherited from Christabel's grandmother – the epidemiologist Dr Alice Stewart.

The modernist kitchen table and chairs were shipped back from an art fair in Turin.

As art dealers, Christabel and Darren feel at home with white spaces. The Welsh blanket is a family heirloom.

Ludo's Lego models are suspended in flight above his bed.

The three-storey staircase rocks a 70s vibe all the way to the top of the house.

essentially six boxes with a staircase through the middle. But it also means you can escape each other when you need to – you can be doing your own thing and not feel on top of each other.'

Whatever floor they are on, it is the warmth and generosity of the building – with its extensive storage space and thoughtful touches such as the bin shelter outside – that really make them feel at home. As Christabel puts it: 'We completely lucked out getting this house.'

Pauline and David's house in Neilston over-looks the giant hump of Neilston Pad – a hill in the Scottish lowlands.

GLASGOW RETRO

When Pauline Clifford and David Meekin bought their ex-council house in Neilston, Glasgow, in 2004, they called in David's dad – an electrician – to help with the rewiring. 'We were pulling old lead cable out of the walls,' recalls David. 'My dad said he hadn't seen anything like it since his apprenticeship. We were drilling into these solid black bricks – there was a lot of bad language that day.'

David and Pauline bought the house from the original tenant, who had been living there since it was built by the then Renfrewshire County Council in 1952. 'Everything was painted black,' remembers Pauline. 'The walls were covered in wood panelling and woodchip wallpaper, and that was all painted black. The carpet did not want to come off the floor. We had to scrub the tiles in the fireplace with a toothbrush to bring them back to life – they were covered in soot and grime.'

The two-bedroom end-of-terrace house has the typical concrete exterior we might all imagine of a council property, with a path to the front door and a jaunty little porch roof. Like so many council homes in village locations, it has jaw-dropping countryside views – overlooking the craggy hunch of Neilston Pad, a large hill which fills the front windows of the house with a canopy of heathery green. 'We see deer grazing out there most mornings,' says Pauline.

They had both been brought up nearby but this was their first home together. 'We were quite young when we moved in, so we've kind of grown up with the house,' explains Pauline. 'At first we were having parties every two weeks – now we've settled down a bit.'

The parties have given way to time spent on their shared love of all things retro, curating their home and their collections of vintage fashion and ephemera. Pauline's dad is

Bold black and white wallpaper and a decorative fireplace packed with candles up the drama stakes in the living room.

A 1950s wing-back chair handed down from Pauline's grandmother gets the kitsch treatment with a leopard-skin seat cover.

David's collection of Tiki mugs is housed in a cabinet handed down from Pauline's grandmother.

The second bedroom has become Pauline's own 'pretend shop' where she keeps her collection of vintage clothes, shoes and bags.

Pink prevails in the bedroom where Pauline's collection of kitsch jewellery is lovingly displayed and a selection of mirrors from her dad's antique shop adorns the wall.

an antique dealer, so her childhood was spent surrounded by old things, on the hunt for bargains at car boot sales and in charity shops. Her dad now runs Clifford Antiques in Los Angeles and she and David are his scouts in Scotland, regularly shipping containers of furniture and collectibles to their mid-century-hungry Californian client base. Pauline, who dresses in bold 1950s style – think circle skirt and cinched waist, flicked eyeliner and a 'poodle' hairdo – also collects vintage clothes and accessories, and has filled the entire second bedroom with her hauls. 'It's like my own wee pretend shop up there.'

David's collections take up less space but are equally rooted in 1950s and '60s nostalgia. On a trip to the US, the couple entered a vintage swimsuit competition at the Viva Las Vegas Rockabilly weekend. David came second (in a vintage Shaheen Cabana set), and won a hand-carved, miniature cocktail

cabinet which is on display in the kitchen. On the same trip, he was the designated driver on the way home, and was given a Tiki mug, crafted and signed by the world's expert on Polynesian pop culture, Sven Kirsten. The prize set David off on his own collecting journey and he now has a number of Tiki mugs – large ceramic drinking vessels depicting imagery from Polynesia and Micronesia – displayed in the living room, in a glass-fronted cabinet which Pauline inherited from her grandmother.

'A lot of the furniture is from my granny's, so it all means a lot and feels familiar to me. I can remember sitting on the armchair in the lounge (which I've covered in leopard skin), and I love the starburst clock.'

Showing off their treasures is at the heart of their home and every room boasts detailed and thoughtfully arranged displays. They chose a black-and-white print wallpaper in the living room so that they could add

The pair take joy in the
art of display every-
where – even around the
kitchen sink.

The original bath and taps are given the fifities look with a black and white tiled floor.

colour and change things around easily. 'We like to look at our things,' says Pauline. 'It brings back memories of places we've been, or who gave it to you. Our families know we like retro stuff, so relatives are always giving us bits, and picking up things in charity shops for us.' Even in the kitchen, where space is tight, there are little vignettes: teapots and a Teasmade, turquoise blinds that coordinate with the washing-up bowl and a box of vintage dominoes.

On the surface it's a house full of colour and kitsch, but beneath the obvious visual markers, there's a sense of sheer joy in the things they possess and an optimism about the journey they are on together. The pair are hoping eventually to move to Los Angeles to work with Pauline's dad, but for now they love the warmth and the friendliness of their 'wee nest' away from the buzz of the city.

'Living in Neilston can feel small. Everybody knows each other – they all seem to know your business. But we've grown up here, we're part of a real community. We feel really cosy here – it's just enough for us.'

TRELLICK TOWER POWER

For Bella Huddart, her flat on the sixteenth floor of Trellick Tower in London's Notting Hill is more than a place to live: it's a symbol of her liberation from a very different sort of life. Married at twenty-three, with six children by the time she was thirty-seven, she had been the consummate country wife for two decades, living in the old rectory of a picturesque Essex village, her home replete with swag curtains, plush carpets and the compulsory Aga.

When she and her husband divorced, Bella – now fifty-one, an interior designer and part-time travel guide – used the settlement money to help buy her first ex-council property in nearby Ledbury Road. 'It was the first property I had ever owned myself. I still had two children at home and four children at university – I had to have a place that would house them all. I put double beds in every room and built a cupboard bedroom, which meant all seven of us could sleep

there. It was an amazing house that really withstood a pummelling from the children.'

She recalls how some friends found her apparent fall from grace hard to swallow: 'Some of them wouldn't come round – they said they'd rather take me out for tea than come in. I think they thought it wasn't safe.'

But for Bella the ex-council house in Ledbury Road was the beginning of a love affair with the architecture and lifestyle of social housing ('It's social housing, it's built for being social in') and when the opportunity came to buy the flat in Trellick Tower she leapt at it. It had been her original plan to let the flat out, but she was so smitten – and by that time almost all her children had homes of their own – that she decided to live there herself along with her youngest son, Eddie.

'People said the lifts never worked and there were all sorts of terrible stories about the crime and what an eyesore it was. But my gut made me disinclined to engage in that. I've always done everything with my gut. If it feels good then I go for it. The lifts do have a life of their own and the rubbish chutes are a problem as they are too small, but there's a great mix of people here and I have lovely relationships with everyone. I really do feel very safe.'

While the flat is a far cry from the country-lady house she once called home, it's heart-warming that she has brought much of the look and feel of her former home with her – 'It's kind of shabby chic meets council house' – so that it seems less a severance from her former life than a new, urban chapter in her fascinating story.

It's certainly hard to imagine there's another flat here with an interior stylistically so at odds with the bones of the building. Trellick is the poster-girl for British brutalism, the sister building to Ernö Goldfinger's Balfron Tower (featured on pages 57–65), with the same distinctive service tower and connecting walkways. Built in 1972 by the GLC, it is Grade II listed, and a star of popular culture: Trellick has appeared in a number of films including *Never Let Me Go* and *Shopping*, as well as music videos by Blur, Gorillaz and others. Its boxy, angular profile is 98 metres of pure grey-brown concrete, looming over the west London skyline.

Yet close the door behind you at Bella's and you are immediately immersed in the whimsy of a soft and feminine temple to shabby chic. The first things you see as you walk up the stairs to the landing are old French mirrors on the wall, little monchrome etchings draped in delicate fairy lights and an elegant iron chandelier overhead. But slicing through the good taste and the prettiness is a huge black-and-white picture of a sexy girl in stockings and a burkha by the female street artist Bambi (often referred to as the 'female Banksy'). 'I got it at Julian Hartnoll's gallery. I like to buy paintings and art when I can afford it,' she says. 'I drag all

A painting by Bambi – known as the female Banksy – hangs over the stairs.

*Much of Bella's furniture has a country-house feel,
having been handed down to her from her family.*

Bella's bedroom is cosy and feminine, with heavy floral curtains and a thick animal-skin rug on the bed. 'It's like being in a womb.'

my paintings around with me wherever I go.'

All the rooms come off this central landing. To the right is the living room, with floor-to-ceiling windows onto the balcony that runs across the front of the flat. While the views which stretch out over the city are uncompromisingly urban, inside feels more like a rural pile in miniature – an effect enhanced by her piano, covered in sheet music and paintings of herself from when she was a life model. 'I had to sell my grand piano, which broke my heart,' she recalls, 'but I managed to keep this one. The removal men who brought it up here said it would never leave the building again and I rather like that idea.' The walls are painted in a washed-out chalky grey and the green velvet corduroy sofa was in her parents' house when she was a little girl. 'It's really granny-ish. I just love the faded grandeur of it.'

Opposite the living room is her bedroom, painted in pretty pinks and lilacs.

There's not much space: the large iron bedstead takes centre stage, the walls are hung with pictures by her son and at the window there are hyper-traditional, thick floral curtains with heavy pelmets. 'It's a bit like being in a womb in here. I love how quiet and small it is. And yet when I look out of the window I can see every form of transport: the cars on the Westway, the trains out of Westbourne Park, even the canal with the houseboats. It's all happening right there.' Next door is her thirteen-year-old son Eddie's room. 'I wanted it to be like a crow's nest – we're so high up – so I put shiplap timber on the wall and painted it blue.' There are more heavy floral curtains brought from her old house. 'Eddie didn't like them at first but I think they are quite reassuring for him. He loves his room and he likes the street element of living here. His friends come round all the time. It seemed like we had hundreds here for Notting Hill Carnival

Old French window shutters replace a full-length door on the bathroom (the toilet is separate).

Bevelled-edge mirrors bounce the light around in the aquamarine bathroom, creating a jewel-like sensation.

last year. If you love this area, everybody loves you.'

Next door in the little bathroom she's used more mirrors to open up the space – the huge faceted one over the sink refracts the light and tones of aquamarine, so it's like standing at the centre of a gemstone. She's done away with unnecessary doors and replaced them with old window shutters: 'I didn't want to be sealed in the bathroom by solid doors.'

It's in the kitchen that her backstory as country-lady-turned-urbanista is most clearly told. The rustic oak table and high-backed chairs are at its centre: 'I grew up with this kitchen table, in Sussex, and it was my dining-room table in Essex. My children said I shouldn't have it in here but I have managed to keep it. I am a great reuser of stuff. The chairs were in my dining room in Essex – they're covered in fabric by Colefax.'

When she moved in, the flat had been occupied by the same tenant since the seventies so the kitchen cupboards and sink were in their original state. 'I took off all the doors and I want to have them stripped and put back on but I can't afford to at the moment. So I've just left them open for now and I've put these little pelmets with cherries on that I found in France along the shelves. I'm keen on things that remind you of places you've been, a sunray you've soaked up.'

The whole look and feel might at first seem incongruous within its brutalist context and yet as Bella points out, Goldfinger was a fan of mixing colours and texture, old and new – just as she has done. 'I've been to his house in Willow Road (a National Trust property) and he had an obsession with mixing stuff up. He loved fabrics and rough paint finishes and textures. Just look at the mix of pebbledash and lino and tiles here in the corridors outside. It's not so different when you think about it.'

A fabric runner with little cherries on, picked up at a French market, brings new life to the plain white carcasses of fitted kitchen cupboards.

Bella grew up around the circular kitchen table and was adamant it would come with her to Trellick, despite objections from her children.

Bella's shabby chic baskets and cushions contrast with the urban cityscape from her balcony.

But for Bella the life she has here at Trellick Tower is not really about the architecture or the way she has furnished the rooms. It's about empowerment and the freedom to be who she wants to be. 'It is so liberating, sitting here on my balcony. I love the bravery of this building. It speaks to me and my personal space. It's what I rescued from the ashes of my marriage. It has given me the freedom to do what I want and liberation from the chains that bound me to a traditional, English married woman's life for so long. It's my friend.'

The modernist lines and a generous front garden of my house in Bridport caught my eye.

The houses in my terrace were all built with concrete posts for the washing line and fruit trees planted at the bottom of the garden (mine now obscured by the kids' trampoline). The views stretch over the town and Colmer's Hill in the distance.

HOME SWEET HOME

I have chosen to feature my own house, not because I consider myself a home-style connoisseur, but because living here was what inspired me to think about other ex-council properties and, ultimately, to write this book. I feel it embodies the idea behind the book – that as a generation of home-buyers we are reassessing our attitudes towards, and redefining the status of, the ex-council home.

My family and I had been looking for a home in Bridport, Dorset, for a while; we wanted to be near relatives who lived there. At the time my son Stanley was a one-year-old, but house prices in the town were – and still are – beyond the reach of many young families. Bridport was becoming popular with out-of-towners looking for a new life by the sea and even with the equity loan we'd been lucky enough to secure from a Homebuy scheme, finding somewhere to live, which was within budget and would suit a growing family, was proving difficult.

I remember seeing the estate agent's details for our house a number of times and passing over them. My eye was caught by the building's vaguely modernist lines, but it had a sullen, dirty concrete exterior (we later painted it to brighten it up) that stopped me giving it proper consideration. It's interesting how, in a rural setting, it is harder to forgive an ugly exterior than it is in the grittier urban sprawl. All my reservations melted away, however, when I viewed the house.

An ample hallway – ideal for the push-chairs and nappy bags and snowsuits that were part of my life at that stage – led to a good-sized living room and spacious kitchen with utility room. Upstairs were three bedrooms – two double and a single – and a reasonable-size bathroom. With built-in storage in both bedrooms and an under- stairs cupboard that satisfied all my larder-based

Blocking up a door between the kitchen and the living room made it possible to turn the kitchen around and showcase the view over Colmer's Hill from the back of the house.

fantasies, it was already trouncing the cardboard-box houses with their stingy rooms and flimsy walls that we'd been looking at until then. But it was the garden that really swung it. Long and wide with a gentle slope, it was three times the size of some of the gardens in other houses we'd been looking at, with views stretching over Bridport and iconic Colmer's Hill in the distance. At the front too there was a decent garden, and with the house set back from the lane by a little path it seemed very private and secluded. It felt – and still does feel – like a house with big welcoming smile on its face.

Like so many homes built by councils in the 1950s, the house has shifted from the hands of the local authority through various housing associations until it was sold into private ownership in the 1990s, and it has been impossible to find out who designed it. I like to imagine the architect was a good host in his or her own home; it feels as though our house was conceived by someone warm, who really considered the needs of the people living there. That's why I wanted to keep the four concrete posts for washing lines in the garden – providing them, along with the fruit trees planted at the bottom of every garden in the terrace, seems like such a thoughtful touch.

It's also why structurally not much has changed: the original build already made the most of the space. It would have been foolish not to do more with the views – which presumably would have been less extraordinary to locals sixty years ago – so a simple patio was put in, with the basic concrete squares that seemed to fit with the house, as well as being the most affordable option. It felt important not to over-spec the place into something it wasn't. Switching the kitchen around to allow for doors onto the patio means that now in the summer it's an

Mid-century colours felt like the right choice for the house, which was built in the 1950s.

The built-in cupboard in Stanley's room (hidden cleverly in the wall) makes use of the cavity above the stairs and joins up with the built-in wardrobe in my room.

extension of the kitchen, where we eat and the kids ride their scooters and generally make a mess.

Style-wise, I've gone for mid-century colours – teal and olive green and mustard yellow – as they seemed to fit with the house's 1950s roots. I'm the first to admit that there's too much grey – Generation X's own magnolia. I paid £5 for the 50s red front door which I found at the tip (to replace a nasty UPVC one with fake stained glass) and put a fififties-style black-and-white tiled floor in the hall. I picked up pieces of old furniture in Bridport's vintage quarter, like the bedside tables with atomic legs, the Ercol chairs and teak coffee table in the lounge, which rub shoulders with modern chests of drawers, sofas and kitchen cupboards. I've collected fifties and sixties things for years but once you have a family you realise that your cool, retro kitchen storage and your elegant dressing table might look the business, but they just don't stand up to the demands of modern family living – the drawers are too small, the cupboards not deep enough.

So it's a house of style compromises, as any family home is, but one I feel I've been able to dress up however the fancy has taken me. Almost everyone I've interviewed for this book says the same thing: that the simple, unembellished spaces of a council home give you the freedom to paint your canvas in a way it would be impossible to do in Edwardian or Victorian properties. This may not be a forever home – my suburban urges for driveways and garages are hard to suppress – but I will always love it, for its kind and generous spirit, for inspiring this book and for the special times I have had here with my family.

I may have overdone it on the grey front, but it is very handy for offsetting other more colourful bits, such as the pink Art Deco mirror in the bathroom.

THANK YOU

So many people have helped to make this book happen. Thank you to Wayne Hemingway, MBE, who went out of his way for a complete stranger, and who shows us what it really means to have a social conscience. To Ros Byam Shaw, queen of the interiors book, who took the time to teach me her art and gave such valuable advice and encouragement. And to Catherine Croft, Director of the Twentieth Century Society, for giving me a crash course in the architecture of social housing and connecting me with so many useful people. To Alex Manson-Smith, for putting me up and putting up with me so many times this past year, and for being my general sounding board. To Rhia Thomas, for her meticulous research into the bilges of retro council paperwork. And to Deborah Shilling, for making some perfectly pitched introductions and being perennially thoughtful. And to everyone who tipped me off, introduced me to people and generally lent a hand finding the houses in this book. To Rosemary Davidson at Square Peg for taking a punt on me and pulling together a brilliant team; to Sarah Cuttle for bringing every home to life so cleverly and being great company on the journey; and to Friederike Huber for designing a book so elegant, I can't quite believe my name is on the front. Finally to Tom Woodhouse, for being the rock our children needed, while I swanned off to ex-council houses across the land. You are all lovely. Thank you.

FURTHER READING

Estates: An Intimate History, Lynsey Hanley: Granta Books, 2007

Council Housing and Culture: The History of a Social Experiment, Alison Ravetz: Routledge, 2001

Modernist Estate: The buildings and the people who live in them, Stefi Orazi: Frances Lincoln, 2015

Concretopia: A Journey Around the Rebuilding of Postwar Britain, John Grindrod: Old Street Publishing, 2013

Housing the Twentieth Century Nation, edited by Elain Harwood and Alan Powers: Twentieth Century Society, 2008

WEBSITES FEATURING
(EX-) LOCAL AUTHORITY HOMES

modernistestates.com

themodernhouse.net

lovelondoncouncilhousing.com

thisbrutalhouse.com

ARCHITECTURE AND DESIGN

Twentieth Century Society
c20society.org.uk

Royal Institute of British Architects
architecture.com

The Geffrye Museum:
Museum of the Home
geffrye-museum.org.uk

Hemingway Design
hemingwaydesign.co.uk

PEOPLE FEATURED IN THIS BOOK

Fiona Gall
emeraldfaerie.com

Harriet Higgins
tattydevine.com

Haidee Drew
haideedrew.com

Mellis Haward
buchananpartnership.com

Kevin Macey
kevinmacey.co.uk

Jane Petrie
janepetrie.com

Pete Reddy
thisareredmanaka.com

Pauline Clifford
cliffordantiques.com

Bow Arts
bowarts.org

Melted Snow
meltedsnow.net

Sarah Thompson
sarahgthompson.com

Sarah Cuttle
sarahcuttle.co.uk

Dan Higgins
dan-higgins.com

10 9 8 7 6 5 4 3 2 1

Square Peg, an imprint of Vintage,
20 Vauxhall Bridge Road,
London SW1V 2SA

Square Peg is part of the Penguin Random House
group of companies whose addresses can be found at
global.penguinrandomhouse.com.

Penguin
Random House
UK

First published by Square Peg in 2015

www.vintage-books.co.uk

A CIP catalogue record for this book is available from
the British Library

ISBN 9780224101134

Penguin Random House is committed to a sustainable
future for our business, our readers and our planet.
This book is made from Forest Stewardship Council®
certified paper.

MIX
Paper from
responsible sources
FSC® C018179

Printed and bound in China by
Toppan Leefung Ltd.